The *New* Insider's Guide to the Best Beaches of The Big Island Hawaii

Newly Revised 2019 with Maps and Complete Directions!

By Uldra Johnson

Copyright 2013 by Uldra Johnson
Revised 2019

This book may not be reproduced, electronically or otherwise, without the written permission of the author.

Cover photograph "Hapuna" by Uldra Johnson

Kai Ka Nani!
(Oh, the sea, how beautiful!)

Aloha, e komo mai!

Welcome to the Big Island, one of the most spectacular places on planet Earth!

If you are coming to Hawaii to bask in the sand in the isle's glorious sunshine, if you are coming to swim in the isle's crystal clear waters, ranging from turquoise to emerald green to sapphire shades of blue, if you are coming to snorkel or dive among its kaleidoscopic, technicolor marine life, you've come to the right place! Here you will find the top 22 beaches on this island, ranked by a beach lover, a beach connoisseur, who knows well the beaches of this magical isle.

From a remote secluded beach at the bottom of the world's most active volcano, which can be accessed only by hiking a desolate frozen lava trail, to a white sand, crescent-moon beach with a 5-star hotel designated one of the five most beautiful beaches in the world, you'll find the beach of *your* dreams here. Want to camp on a rugged beach in an uninhabited valley, and sleep to the sound of wild surf? Want to sit atop a sugary white sand dune and watch silvery dolphins leap from turquoise waters into the golden sky in the diamond sunshine? Or maybe you want to swim in an emerald-green bay so close to spinner dolphins that you can hear them joyfully singing to one another?

What about finding the best body and boogie boarding beach in the Islands, where the surf *never* stops rolling, and whose white sands magically disappear and then reappear? Want to go where wild horses run up and down a black sand beach in a valley of waterfalls, some who might be coaxed to take a banana out of your hand? Or would you like to leave your footprints on a bejeweled green sand beach, sparkling with semiprecious stones, on a windswept, steep-cliffed bay, with nothing between you and Antarctica, but the deep blue sea?

This guide, written by a beach lover who came to Hawaii *for* its beaches more than thirty years ago, will take you to these astounding places, and more.

How about snorkeling or scuba diving in the Garden of Eels, and possibly be the first to find one of history's most legendary shipwrecks, rumored to be within swimming distance of the island's shores? How about a beach said to be haunted by Night Marchers, *huaka'i po*, the ghosts of long-dead warrior armies? And then there is the beach named for its springs of life, from whose sacred waters only the royalty of Hawaii were permitted to drink, on pain of death? Would you like to visit the pristine Golden Ponds? What about stepping down into the lovely and alluring Queen's Bath?

What about a beach where Hawaii's greatest queen lived as a girl, on whose shores kings were sacrificed, and where high-born maidens soaked in sacred pools to increase their fertility? Or perhaps your liking is for a more social beach, a *where the girls (or boys) are* sort of beach, where beautiful thong-clad wahines, happy surfers, boogie boarders, skate boarders, and volleyball enthusiasts sport like gods and goddesses in the golden sun?

Want to hike to an unspoiled bay with a nearby lava tube filled with seawater, reachable only by descending into with a ladder? What about a beach where you can learn to surf or take a glass bottom boat ride or para-sail or windsurf? Do you prefer a white, black, or green sand beach, or maybe a beach unique in all the world, a white *and* black sand beach?

Do you want a beach where you can go sky clad? What about a beach with tide pools, ancient ponds, rock formations, and a picturesque lava rock island in the heart of the bay? Want to know where you can see manta rays with wingspans of 30 feet, or dive down and touch the nose of a sleeping shark? Or is your preference for a long, golden-sanded strand where you can run to your heart's content, somersault, dive after Frisbees, do yoga and stand on your head in the soft sand?

It's all here, in *The New Insider's Guide to the Best Beaches of the Big Island Hawaii*!

Ready?

Let's hit the beach!

"If you're lucky enough to be at the beach...then you're lucky enough!"
(Anonymous Saying)

Whoa! Wait a minute! Not so fast! Before we can actually begin, there is a little technicality you should understand. It has to do with finding your away around the Big Island.

Guide to Beaches by Mile-markers

One essential thing to understand is that on the Big Island, we find where we are going by mile-markers! Yes, every mile of the road is marked!

Basically, you can think of one main road following along the coast of the Big Island, forming a circle, called the Hawaiian Belt Road. The Hawaii Belt road consists of Hawaii State Routes 11, 19, and 190. The southern section, between Hilo and Kailua-Kona is Route 11. The section between Hilo and Waimea is Route 19. From Waimea, the road splits; there is an "upper" road, the mauka road, and a "lower" road, the makai road. The lower road, which traces the sea, is a continuation of Route 19. Yes, you need to know these two important Hawaiian words as you travel about—*mauka* and *makai*. *Mauka* means "towards the mountain" and *makai* means "toward the sea."

The mile-markers begin in Hilo at zero, and increase going south, on Route 11, until Palani Road in Kailua-Kona, which is mile-marker #122. They decrease if you reverse direction from Kailua-Kona going toward Hilo.

Traveling north from Hilo, on Route 19, the mile-markers also begin at zero and increase until Palani Road in Hilo.

So there can be two mile-markers #69, but one is on Route 11, and one is on Route 19.

Can be confusing until you get used to it!

Study this map for a moment. You'll get the hang of it.

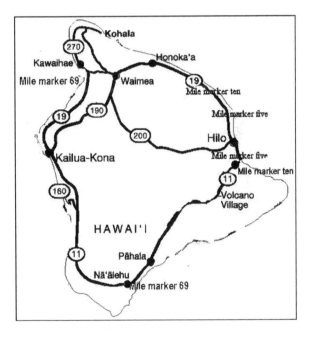

Got it? Now we can get started! So in order of my favorites, here are the best beaches on the Big Island. IMHO!

My Favorite Beaches

From #1-22

Makalawena
Mahai'ula (and Ka'elehuluhulu)
Kua Bay (Manini'owali Beach)
Napo'opo'o Beach at Kealakekua Bay
Manini Beach
Ke'ei Beach
Pu'uhonua o Honaunau
Two-Step Beach (Keone'ele Cove)
Wai'alea (Beach 69 and Beach 67)
Hapuna
Kiholo
Honokohau Beach (The Nude Beach), 'Alula Beach and Ai'opio Beach
Halape
Waipi'o
Kahalu'u
Kauna'oa Beach (Mauna Kea Beach)
Road to the Sea Black Sand Beach (Kaupua'a Beach)
La'aloa (Magic Sands, Disappearing Sands, White Sands)
Pololu Valley Beach
Keawaiki Beach, the Golden Ponds, Pueo Bay and Weliweli Point
Anaeho'omalu Bay (A-Bay, Waikoloa Beach)
Ka Lae (South Point) and Green Sands Beach (Papakolea)

Surf's up! Let's Go!

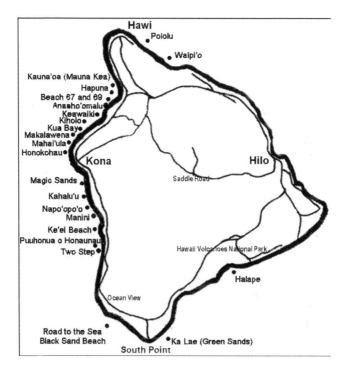

Kekaha Kai State Park and Makalawena

Without a doubt, most of the most beautiful and spectacular beaches on Hawaii Island are along the famed golden Kona Coast. That beach of your dreams, the one with the white sands, swaying palm trees and turquoise waters, the one of beautiful technicolor sunsets and salt sea breezes, actually exists. There is a reason the royalty of Hawaii, the ali'i, spent as much time as possible along this coast —surfing, fishing, playing, relaxing. The Kona coast was their playground. These sun-drenched beaches are a beach-goers paradise, and I am going to introduce you to my favorites, the ones I have returned to again and again, the ones where I have experienced true magic.

The land of Kekaha Kai is shaped by the lava flows of 1800-1801 and 1859. For miles around, all is black congealed lava. The earliest western description of this coast was written by Captain George Vancouver, who sailed past Kekaha Kai in 1794. He wrote, "The shores were uninteresting, being composed chiefly of volcanic matter and producing only a few detached groves of coconut trees, with the appearance of very little cultivation, and very few inhabitants."

Of course, Captain Vancouver probably had very little interest in sunbathing, surfing, swimming, body boarding and other such frivolous activities. He was a man with a mission, and the sea was simply business. He couldn't even swim! How times have changed! How we now seek out such golden shores with few people!

Kekaha Kai State Park, formerly called Kona Coast State Park, encompasses over 1,500 acres of beach, dune and wilderness areas. This park is divided into two sections: **Mahai'ula** and **Kua Bay**, and in between them, is the gem of gems, **Makalawena**, which is, precariously, still privately owned by the Bishop Estate. Mahai'ula Beach is the most developed of the two official state beaches, with picnic tables, trashcans, restrooms, and showers, but no drinking water. Kua Bay, also called Manini'owali, also has these amenities, and in addition, a paved road makes easy access, but also brings in more people. Makalawena is still, thankfully, pristine and completely undeveloped. Unpaved road access between the two State-owned sections, a 4.5-mile hike from Mahai'ula along the Ala Kekaha Kai Trail, a historic coastal trail, leads to the Kua Bay portion of the Park. Halfway along this trail, a hike to the summit of Pu'u Ku'ili, a 342-foot high cinder cone, offers excellent coastline views.

Of course, my *very* favorite of these three beaches is Makalawena, but if you get a chance, visit all three.

I will tell you how to get there!

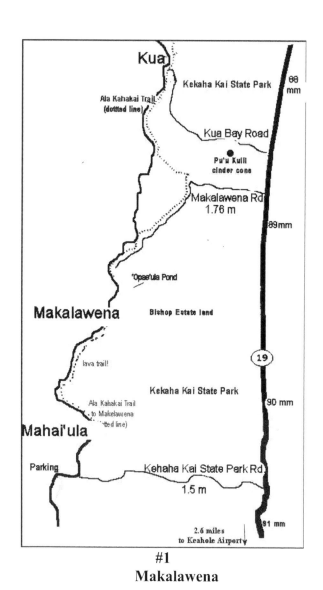

#1
Makalawena

Ah, the jewel of jewels! My all time favorite beach!

Getting there: there are *four* ways to get to Makalawena.

1) For this first option, *if you have 4-wheel drive*, head north from Kailua on Hwy. 19. Two miles past the Kekaha Kai State Park sign, you will see a large, red cinder cone, Pu'u Ku'ili, on the seaside rising from an otherwise flat landscape. You can't miss it. Get ready to turn left, toward the sea, approximately midway between the **88 and 89** mile-markers. *Look closely* for an unmarked dirt road—usually there are a few cars parked here. From here it is a *very* rough 1.75 miles to the beach, through *a'a* lava (the rough stuff) and white coral. Do not even *think* about taking a non-four-wheel drive on this road! At some points you may think the road ends, but keep going all the way; eventually you will come to a locked gate. You must park here (remember, to the side, not in front of Bob's gate), and walk in. You can keep walking past the beautiful singing ironwood grove to the lovely white sand dunes beyond.

While the *mauka-makai* (mountain to sea) trail from Highway 19 has been used by locals for years and in more recent years by increasing numbers of tourists, generally without much objection from Bishop Estate, which owns Makalawena, it *is* crossing private property and the Estate would rather one use the designated hiking trail. Also, keep in mind that if you do drive in on this road**, do not park in front of the gate**, but over to the side. Otherwise, you will feel the full wrath of Makalawena Bob, whose driveway you will be blocking! More about him later!

2) If you *don't* have four-wheel drive, you can follow the above directions to the beginning of the access road on Highway 19, park on the side of the highway, and *walk* the very hot two miles in. Not bad, but remember—it's four miles round trip, and in between is a whole day of activity, so plan your energy accordingly. Also, take *lots* of water!

3) Option three. You can take the turn into Kekaha Kai State Park, which is 2.6 miles north from Keahole airport between mile-markers **90 and 91** (you'll see the sign) and drive in on the rough but doable road, and park. This is Mahai'ula beach, as described below, beautiful in its own right, and you might be tempted to stay here. But to continue on to Makalawena, you walk north along the beach until you see the old, abandoned, red Magoon house, the only house on the beach. You can't miss it. Climb up the steps toward the house, and just in back, through an oasis of palm trees, you will see a distinct trail across the a'a lava—that's the rough stuff—heading north. This is a segment of the Ala Kekaha Kai Trail. This portion of the trail is about a third of a mile, roughly 20 minutes across, to Makalawena. The trail is hot, rough, and you need shoes, though I have hiked it many times in slippahs—just have to watch not to skin the toesies! (The secret to walking safely on lava is in the Hawaiian saying, "Keep your lips zipped and your eyes to the ground.") Remember, the ancient Hawaiians did it barefoot! It's a wonderful trail; the juxtaposition between the large expanses of black lava and the turquoise sea on one side, and the black lava and the mountains on the other, is quite memorable. You are likely to see wild goats along

the way, who look at you rather curiously, wondering how in the world you are managing without hooves.

At the end of the lava trail, you will come out in a grove of kiawe, mesquite trees. Here you definitely need slippahs minimum, as the ground is covered with large, very nasty thorns. Watch your step! There is a story that kiawe was planted to force the natives to wear shoes, but another story is that it was brought here for cattle fodder. This area has a strange, almost acrid smell and is kind of creepy. Keep going and very shortly you will come up behind the sand dunes.

Here you have a wonderful choice. You can climb up to the top of the first sand dune and, once there, feast your eyes on one of the most beautiful sights you will ever see! From the top of the dunes, one of the most magnificent views on the planet opens up. Azure-turquoise waters spread out in the distance, and the powdery white dunes invite you to roll, tumble, or run down into the waves. They'll bring out the inner child in you! This truly is a realm of enchantment. If it's clear, as it usually is, Maui will be visible, and also the ranch lands of the northern part of the island, Kohala. Looking back in the opposite direction, away from the ocean, three volcanoes are visible—Mauna Kea, Mauna Loa, and Hualalai, and in winter, sometimes snow-capped Mauna Loa and Mauna Kea will glisten in the sun.

Or, you can continue on the path below and behind the dunes, which in a short distance, about a fourth of a mile, will take you to a magical oasis, the Queen's Bath. It's what's called an anchialine pond, a type of pond that exists in inland lava depressions near the ocean. These ponds are fed by freshwater springs or from percolation from the water table. The water level in the pond rises about 18-24 inches during high tide or high surf, and is noticeably saltier. After a refreshing dip in the pool, you can then climb over the sand dunes and feast your eyes on your first view of this magnificent beach. *Please do not wear sun screen into the pond!*

In either case, if you walk in, travel lightly. It's usually *very* hot out here. And take plenty of water. I usually just wear a pareo over my bathing suit, and carry water, plus wear sunglasses and a visor. You probably definitely want sunscreen as well.

4) Another option: you can also hike to Makalawena from Kua Bay. Directions to Kua Bay will be given below. From Kua Bay, you hike the Ala Kekaha Kai Trail, about an hour walk.

There is at least one other way, besides boating in.

Once, when I sitting on the sand dunes at Makalawena, a helicopter began to hover noisily overhead. After about five minutes of maneuvering, to my amazement, it alit on the beach in front of me. A man jumped out and then handed down a beautiful woman, who was carrying a picnic basket. The couple spread out a blanket, enjoyed lunch for about thirty minutes, and then packed up again. The man once again handed the beautiful woman into the helicopter, climbed in himself, there was a whirling of wings, and they were off!

Important note: If you park your car at Mahai'ula, and hike to Makalawena, remember that the gate closes at 7 p.m.

Now that you're here...

Ah! Makalawena! The most beautiful beach in the world! And perhaps, even, the most beautiful place I have ever seen on planet Earth. It doesn't get more idyllic than this!

Oh the mystical experiences I have had on this magical beach! The *sensory* experiences! Experiences to cherish!

I promise to tell you about one unforgettable such experience, one that, if you time it just right, you might be able to duplicate for yourself. But first, I'll have to describe this enchanting place.

Picture turquoise crystal waters. Sugary-white sand dunes. Views of the volcanoes to the back of the dunes—sometimes Mauna Kea adorned in a mantle of glistening snow. Maui floating liking an emerald jewel. Gently swerving shoreline all the way to Kohala in the north. Beautiful groves of singing ironwood trees (Casuarina equisetifolia) to retreat to for shade when the sun gets too hot, where you can nap on the soft carpet of their abundant needles. Green sea turtles bobbing their heads up out of the sparkling water. Dolphins leaping like silver coins dropped from the golden sky in the glinting, diamond sunshine. And at certain times of the year, huge black flower petals gently intertwining, swirling, and undulating near the edge of the foaming water—these are giant manta rays.

Makalawena is definitely the jewel of jewels. Want to return to the magical days of childhood? On most days, I'd say 350 sunny days out of the year, mornings at Makalawena will make you feel like a child again, full of laughter, enthusiasm, and joy. Then in the afternoon, if you don't feel inclined to seek the shelter of the peaceful ironwoods while the sun climbs higher and higher, and it gets hotter and hotter, you might want to wrap yourself up, head and all, in your pareo, and wait out the heat in silence and meditation, like an Arab in the desert, while the ball of the sun spins like a gyre on fire.

The inexpressibly lovely beach of Makalawena stretches over five cove/inlets and covers an area of about a mile of perfect shoreline. Want to see every blue in Mother Nature's pallet? From the light electric blues near the shore, to the dark sapphire-blue waters over the coral reef shelf just off shore, to the lavender-blues of the shadows between the sand dunes, they're all here.

The five coves that make up Makalawena are, from north to south, Pohakukohola, Paewa'a, Naili'ili, Lepeamoa, and Pokuloa. Just getting to these lovely coves, whether hiking in or four wheeling it, is a great adventure. You will find few people here, for few choose to take their cars down the *really* rough road, or want to walk the usually grueling hot road in and out. Many times I have had the entire beach to myself. This is a beach, one of the few left, where it is acceptable (not necessarily legal) to go sky clad. Just like a little child again.

Makalawena Beach is one of the last wilderness beaches in all of Polynesia you can backpack into, though camping is legally permitted only by permit from Bishop Estate. But if you are discreet, and *very respectful*, Makalawena Bob, the caretaker, *might* (not saying for sure) allow you to sleep out on the soft sand dunes under the stars, an unforgettable cosmic experience.

Makalawena is a beach lover's dream comes true. Its shores are usually empty, never crowded. Occasionally, very rarely, in fact I have only seen this happen once but I have heard it does happen, boisterous locals take it over on weekends, so it's best to camp there during the week. There are *no* conveniences, like a toilet, so be prepared.

It's hard to find much about Makalawena historically. It is said that the ancient Hawaiians considered it a special healing place, and I believe it. One's soul simply expands when one stands on top of the highest sand dune, and stares out at the sea. The feel of the sea breezes on one's bare skin, the vibrant colors, the sound of the waves, the solitude, the pristine elements of air, water, earth and fire—this is a place where all one's senses peak in enjoyment. Makalawena heals on some sort of animal level.

Makalawena belongs to the Bishop Estate, as does much of the seacoast of the Big Island. Bishop Estate reluctantly, after much pressure, contributed a large section of coastal strip towards the State Park effort; the Makalawena holding continues to be owned by Kamehameha Schools/Bishop Estate, but for how long, who knows.

How this came about is very interesting. Previous to 1848, Hawaii was a semi-feudal system. Under this system, rule over an ahupua'a, a land division extending from the uplands to the sea, was given by the king to a chief, who received taxes and tribute from the people who worked the land collectively. Private land ownership did not exist; a commoner could be expelled from his land by the chief, or the chief removed by the king. Hoping to keep ownership of the land out of the hands of foreigners, in 1848 the king and his 245 chiefs met to divide the Hawaii lands among themselves. This was called the Great Mahele of 1848. Sixty percent of the land was allocated to the crown as the Hawaiian crown lands. Thirty-nine percent was allocated to the chiefs. The remaining one percent went to the commoners. Guess who got the choicest lands?

Makalawena is one of 22 ahupua'a that make up the land division of Kekaha Kai in North Kona. Makalawena ahupua'a was awarded to a great-granddaughter of Keoua Nui, the father of Kamehameha the Great. When she passed away in 1877, she willed Makalawena to her cousin, Bernice Pauahi Bishop. This later became a part of the Kamehameha Schools Trust, upon the death of Bernice Pauahi Bishop in 1884.

Bishop Estate still holds title to all one hundred percent of the property, so it is not within Hawaii State Park boundaries per se. However, the State has identified the property (or sections thereof) for future incorporation as the most desirable alternative for the long-range plan for the Park.

The State has somewhat aggressively asserted rights to the shoreline, beach, any ponds and archeological sites. The historic trail system is basically theirs already.

Makala means to loosen, undo, untie, liberate; it also means to forgive, to free of defilement, to open or unfold, as a flower. *Wena* means glow, like that of a sunrise or fire. So in one sense, *Makalawena* means "suffusing rosy glow," but it could also have a healing connotation—to let oneself loose, to liberate oneself, to unfold oneself, which is what one does when one forgives or is forgiven.

The Hawaiian ancients told legends about every rock, nook and cranny of Hawaii, and there is at least one about Makalawena. In it, Makalawena took its name from a hero named Kamiki, who destroyed evil spirits residing there, by drowning them in the sea. Perhaps this is another variation on the theme of the healing qualities of this beautiful place, a place where negativity is absorbed by the pristine waters.

The legend states that the spirit god Pahulu, whose name means *nightmare*, came with his hoards of ghosts and began to terrorize the inhabitants who at that time lived here. Kamiki, who was a skilled fishermen and warrior, ensnared these ghosts in a supernatural net called Kuʻukuʻu, and took the ghosts and drowned them along the shore of Makalawena. The beach is named *Makalawena* for the eerie glow that came from the sea after the spirits were defeated. It is said that one ghost did escape and continues to haunt this coastline. It's whispered that local fishermen do not speak aloud of setting nets because the ghost will make the sea rough and prevent them from catching any fish.

I have also read that Makalawena means "mischievous winds," in reference to the sometimes-unpredictable gusty winds. The Goddess of Wind, Laʻamaomao, so pissed off the other gods on the Kona coast that one day they surrounded her and cut off her nose, tossing it on the shore by Makalawena

Beach. La'amaomao's nose thus became Pu'u Ku'ili, the 342 feet high cinder cone visible as the tallest landmark in the area. Now, the wind goddess no longer troubles the other gods but the mischievous winds of La'amaomao still sometimes play around Pu'u Ku'ili and Makalawena. I have been there on such a windy day. If you happen to go there on such a day, you can take shelter behind the sand dunes, in the Queen's Bath, which will be described below, or in the large rocks that jut out into the sea.

The lava flows that make up Makalawena came down from Hualalai volcano from a cinder cone called Huehue. The lava flows are between 5,000 and 10,000 years old. Both *a'a*, the sharp-as-glass lava, and *pahoehoe*, the smooth, ribbon-like lava, make up the landscape at Makalawena.

You wouldn't believe it now, as you relish the solitude of this beautiful place, but there was once a settlement here. In 1867, a school and church was established with a school class of 16 students. Wow! Wouldn't you have liked to have been one of those students! By 1898, there were 32 children attending this school, and the village consisted of a store and nine hale (houses). By 1920, most of the families had left Makalawena and the school was, unfortunately, closed. The 1946 tsunami wiped out the remainder of the settlement and it was never rebuilt.

Back in the eighties, when I first discovered Makalawena, there was one lone resident, an old fisherman with a shack right on the edge of the beach, who kept goats and chickens. After him, the Bishop Estate, which holds the lands around the beach, hired Bob as caretaker, whose principle job is to keep goats from overrunning the area and ensure that the proper respect is paid to this natural wonder. That's Bob's colorful shack you see just yards from the beach. If you're lucky, you might get to meet him. If you are really lucky, you might get to hear him sing and strum his guitar as the sun sets and the stars come out. He's as colorful and interesting as his shack, but don't misbehave; underneath his easy-going manner is a guy who can really do his job. He'll boot out those who are disrespectful of the *aina* (the land).

So here is a good place to say it. Makalawena is an atypically fragile biosystem even for Kona, so *please be clean and careful. Pack out your garbage; leave no footprints*, except the ones in the sand.

Makalawena ahupua'a stretches about five miles up Hualalai Mountain to Akahipu'u hill. The north boundary of Makalawena ahupua'a is named Inenui rock at Pohakuiwikohola Point. The south boundary is a *kaheka* (tide pool) called Kaelemiha. The center of Makalawena is a large sand dune named Pu'uali'i, which means "ali'i hill." It runs *mauka* (toward the mountains) of the beach along the shoreline. The bay is about 0.8 miles across, from one side to the other.

You'll probably want to swim just below Pu'uali'i, where the sand dunes are the highest, which is the middle of the beach. This is Pu'uali'i Beach. The gently sloping shallow waters here are perfect for body boarding (especially in winter when the waves are up) or just lying on your back in the perfect water or on the sand and staring up into the perfect sky. Snorkeling is fabulous here too. I have witnessed lovers making love here too, in the evening when no one else was around—I guess they just couldn't help themselves. Not to blame!

Walk up and over the *pohuehue*-draped sand dunes of Pu'uali'i—pohuehue are the beautiful purple morning glory vines—and you will find the path to the lovely Queen's Bath, also known as the Goddess Pool, a beautiful green and blue pool of refreshing water fit for a queen. Lovely beyond words, it's a pool of sapphire blue water hidden in the black lava and surrounded by coconut palms. Looking down onto it always reminds me of pictures of planet Earth taken from outer space. This is a mostly freshwater and brackish pond hidden down in the lava where you can seclude yourself even further and rinse off. Curious little red shrimp, brine shrimp, may nibble on our toes and fingers; don't worry, they are harmless. Again, please do not wear lotion into the water.

Also behind Pu'uali'i, just slightly north of the Queen's Bath, is one of the Island's most important sanctuaries for water birds. It is listed as a National Natural Landmark. 'Opae'ula Pond was once an ancient Hawaiian fish pond—you can now watch stilts, coots and ducks on this 12 acre sanctuary. The pond is named for the 'opae'ula, the tiny red shrimp which the Hawaiians used to use for bait for 'opelu, a type of mackerel; the shrimp is also food for the water birds.

This pond is the most important site for the endangered a'eo, the Hawaiian Stilt (*Himantopus knudseni*). A tall, slender, wading bird with white on its face, neck, and stomach, and black on its head, the stilt is an endangered species and it is endemic to the Hawaiian Islands. The stilt has a long, black bill measuring approximately three inches. It can grow to be 16 inches in length. The males are black in color and the females are a brownish color. Its distinctive feature is its long pinkish-red legs that make it look like it is walking on stilts.

Other birds to see here are the *'auku'u*, the black-crowned night heron *(Nycticorax nycticorax hoactli)*, the *'alae ke'oke'o* (Hawaiian Coot, *Fulica ala)*, wandering tattlers, golden plovers, doves and cardinals. The night heron, whose only known breeding ground is here, is one of my favorite birds; for years, when I worked as a gardener in Kona, one solitary heron would come each year for a few weeks and visit our pond. He would sit unblinking for hours on a rock in the middle of the pond, fishing. Talk about being lost in meditation! I always felt sorry for him, because I knew there were no fish in that pond. I got a treasured photo of him.

Other critters you will see here are: Franklin Sand crabs, *a'ama* crabs, *moa* (chickens), *Kao* (goats, there is a magnificent herd with a great white Billy goat known as "King"), *O'opu*, *Hauke'uke* (the fleshy, faceted-looking urchin), *Kupe'e,* and edible shellfish. Kupe'e live in sand and under the sand and among the rocks. At night the kupe'e come out of the sand and feed on plant algae found on the rock surface. Their shells were formerly treasured as bracelets.

You'll often see *Honu* (green sea turtles), and *Manini*, the beautiful light-greenish fish with the six black stripes running down the body, are found along most shorelines in Hawaii. Their young are often found in tide pools and at the waters edge. Manini are often seen in large schools grazing on the reef—if you get the chance to see them graze, look for other territorial fish trying to scare them away. They are also a sight to see while traveling in great numbers, resembling a parade making its way along the reef. It's fun to snorkel along with a school of Manini.

Out on the rocks you'll see *opihi*. Opihi are snails that live on wave-swept rocks in intertidal and shallow-water areas. Also called limpets, opihi shells look like Chinese straw hats. Such broad-based shells offer minimum water resistance to the powerful blasts of water that come regularly from breaking waves. They are a traditional Hawaiian food but, due to increasing scarcity, are becoming a delicacy.

The strong opihi shells also protect the animal when clamped down on its rock home. And these snails can really hang on tight! Unless you sneak up on these critters when they're relaxed, there's little hope of prying them off with bare hands. But please, don't! Live and let live.

Pipipi, the little black snails with the spiral grooves, are well named. The Hawaiian word means "small and close together," and that's how most of these half-inch-long snails spend their days—crowded together under ledges or in depressions of Hawaii's rocky shorelines. Ancient Hawaiians prized these shells, using them in bracelets and leis. Hawaiians ate all species of these snails, sometimes raw, sometimes heating them, then plucking the snail from its shell with a sharp stick.

The *'akekeke*, or Ruddy Turnstone, is a dramatically colored shorebird with short orange legs, variegated russet color pattern on its back, and black and white head, throat, neck and breast. This stocky shorebird is medium in size and distinguishable in flight by its white back, rump, upper tail coverts, wing bar and patch on the inner wing. It is an indigenous bird found in the winter months on rocky beaches of Hawaii and other tropical Pacific coasts. They are called Turnstones because they turn stones over with their beaks to find and eat the small insects and crustaceans underneath.

In Hawaiian mythology the 'akekeke is a messenger of the gods sent across the ocean to carry missives to other islands. In one legend, the bird was sent to warn and protect Princess Paliuli, when Prince Aiwahi tried to destroy her.

You might see another bird, the *koloa*, the Hawaiian duck. They have been considered endangered since 1978. However, all the Hawaiian ducks in the reestablished populations have bred with feral Mallard ducks and have produced hybrid offspring that are fully fertile. In legend, the koloa birds protected a blind giant warrior, Ima-i-ka-lani, and quacked to warn him from which side he might be attacked.

Kolea is the Hawaiian name for the Pacific Golden Plover. The kolea is an important bird in Hawaiian chants and hula. Kolea means "one who takes and leaves." The Pacific Golden Plover (Pluvialis dominica fulva) or the kolea, is a migratory bird; it breeds along the coast of Western Alaska and Siberia. It spends its winters in Hawaii and in places throughout the South Pacific and Indian Oceans. The kolea's plumage changes color. During the spring, in

Hawaii, the top is black with white and golden, yellow spots.

The cute name "puhi" sounds innocuous enough, but is the word for the rather scary looking bony fish, the eel. The Hawaiian Islands are home to eels from three families. Eels are generally not aggressive toward swimmers or divers, who usually only get bit if they reach into a cave or hole in the reef, surprising or threatening an eel. This may result in a severe cut, especially if the hand is jerked back rapidly when it is bitten as this may increase the damage done by the eel's backward-pointing teeth. It's like trying to back your car out over one of those steel-toothed traffic guards. I met a woman on the beach once, not at Makalawena, who just been bitten by an eel. She showed me the wound on her finger. She was scared more than hurt. She said she had reached into a little hole where a brightly colored snail sat, and the eel, hidden in the hole, had lunged out and latched on to her fingers. I suppose he considered the snail his.

In ancient Hawaii some eels were considered *aumakua*, spiritual guardians, and there are many sayings about eels.

He puhi ke aloha, he iʻa noho I ke ale.

"Love is like an eel, the creature that dwells in the sea cavern," which means, "Love makes one restless in the mind, like the writhing of an eel."

He puhi kumu one, he iʻa ʻino.

"An eel of the sand bank is a dangerous creature," said of eels that can travel on the sand and rocks. This was said of a dangerous person.

Tales are told of eels climbing pandanus trees and dropping on persons resting or sleeping under them. Whether or not eels can travel on the sand and rocks I don't know, but I think it could be true.

I remember once sitting out by the water near the Kona Inn, in Kailua town. As I placidly ate my lunch, I watched three giant, I mean *giant*, about ten foot long, eels, fight in between the rocks on the sandy beach. The water was only inches high; basically, the eels were gliding about on the sand and over the rocks. It was a sight to remember, and they were ferocious, like ghastly monsters fighting to the death. I can tell you, after that, I am not one to hang about and watch eels while in the water.

Morays eels love rocky areas and can be found living or just hanging out in holes, under rocks, crevices and tide pool ledges. If you snorkel around the rocks at Makalawena, you most probably will see some. To prevent contact and possible severe injury, keep your hands out of those rocky areas, holes and crevices. If you must, use a stick to probe. If you are fishing, be careful, as dead fish, blood or bait will bring them out of their holes.

They injure you with their razor sharp teeth and powerful jaws that allegedly can lock. Injuries can result in bleeding, severe muscle damage, or also chipped bones. Stop any bleeding with pressure and clean wounds thoroughly. Get medical help for severe wounds.

Wana, urchins, are those interesting sea creatures in the echinoderm family that look like balls with spines covering them. They can be dangerous because they shoot out their spines, which have toxin in them. Sea urchins live in rocks and live under rocks and creep and crawl by sliding with their tube feet. There are the purplish-black wana, and the larger red wana.

Sea urchins are a minor threat while snorkeling. The most dangerous urchins have thin needle-like spines that are venomous. However, all urchins can injure your feet if you step on them.

Protect yourself while snorkeling by following a simple set of precautions. Wear water shoes or flippers during your snorkeling, or do as I do—I never put my feet on the floor of the ocean, and if I stand on rocks, I LOOK first. If you must stand, inspect the area before you place your foot down.

Wana are gathered with the aid of a stick to avoid wounds from the spines. Gathered seasonally, wana are considered the most delicious delicacy. To eat them, their spines are knocked off with a stone or stick, the wana are opened by crushing or by putting salt into their mouths and leaving it overnight to make cracks around the mouth form. The five orangey tongues of the gonads, the meat most prized by Hawaiians, are then scooped out. The Hawaiians consume the fluid from the body cavity and mouth, sometimes using it in a relish to eat with poi or sweet potatoes. Hawaiians also eat the wana eggs.

Not my cup of tea! (I'm a confirmed vegetarian.)

Makalawena is one of the most pristine ecosystems on the island. You may enjoy looking closely at the flora here.

Plants of this area are *kiawe* (Mesquite), fountain grass, pohuehue, *kaunaoa*, *niu* (coconut), and limu (seaweed, of which there are many varieties).

You'll know kiawe by its treacherous thorns, of course. The lovely pinkish-golden fountain grass, an invasive from South Africa, brought to Hawaii as an ornamental, is appropriately named and easily identified. I've already mentioned the beach morning glory, pohuehue. Kaunaoa is an air plant that is a parasitic twining vine. The yellow and orange strands that grow from the vine are used in lei making, and make exquisite and prized leis. The yellowish flowers of the plant grow in tiny clusters long the stems and are only 1/16 of an inch. You might find it growing entwined with the pohuehue.

Legend has it that, long ago, Pohuehue and Kaunaoa were two lovers. Pohuehue and Kaunaoa were the best of friends and deeply in love; however one day they got in an argument. Pohuehue got so angry he sailed away to live on another island. One morning while thinking of his lost lover, Pohuehue began picking hau blossoms (native yellow hibiscus) and tossing them into the waves. The flowers drifted to the beach where Kaunaoa sat, also thinking of her lost love. Upon seeing the flowers, Kaunaoa followed them across the water and back into Pohuehue's arms, where the two still embrace. Kaunaoa is recognized as the flower lei material of Lana'i Island.

You also find coconut trees around the Queen's Bath; I think Makalawena Bob planted them.

The *naupaka Kekaha Kai* plant that you will see at Makalawena is one of eight types of Hawaiian naupaka—and the only one that can be found elsewhere in the world. The name naupaka Kekaha Kai literally means *naupaka by the sea* and you will see lots of it at Makalawena.

The naupaka Kekaha Kai has thick pulpy leaves that are a light green color. Leaves cluster outward from the stem. The flowers are small and whitish flowers with light purple streaks; they are interesting because they have petals only on the lower half of the flower. While the plant can grow up to 10 feet, most stands are wider than they are tall—up to 15 to 20 feet wide and thick and 3 to 5 feet tall.

Another type of naupaka grows in the mountains. The flower looks identical to the naupaka Kekaha Kai but the extensions are only on the upper half, just the opposite from the naupaka Kekaha Kai. There is a legend to account for this.

Two young lovers, greatly devoted to each other, came to the attention of Goddess Pele. Pele found the young man desirable and appeared before him as a beautiful stranger. But no matter how Pele wooed him, the lovers remained devoted to each other.

Enraged, Pele chased the young man into the mountains, throwing molten lava at him. Pele's sisters witnessed this and, to save the young man from certain death, they changed him into the mountain naupaka. Pele immediately went after the young woman and chased her towards the sea, but again Pele's sisters stepped in and changed the young lover into beach naupaka.

It is said that if the mountain naupaka and beach naupaka flowers are reunited, the two young lovers will be together again

Another version goes like so. Naupaka was a beautiful Hawaiian princess. Her parents approached Naupaka and asked her what was troubling her.

"I have fallen in love with a man named Kaui," replied the princess. "But Kaui is not of noble birth—he is a commoner."

According to Hawaiian tradition, you see, it was strictly forbidden for members of royalty to marry people from the common ranks.

Sadly, Naupaka and Kaui traveled long and far, seeking a solution to their dilemma. They climbed up a mountain to see a *kahuna* who was staying at a heiau (temple), but he had no clear answer for the young lovers.

"There is nothing I can do," he told them, "but you should pray. Pray at this heiau."

So they did. And as they prayed, rain began to fall. Their hearts torn by sorrow, Naupaka and Kaui embraced for a final time. Then Naupaka took a flower from her ear and tore it in half, giving one-half to Kaui.

"The gods won't allow us to be together," she said. "You go live down by the water, while I will stay up here in the mountains."

As the two lovers separated, the naupaka plants that grew nearby saw how sad they were. The very next day, they began to bloom in only half flowers.

The *'akulikuli plant*, (Sesuvium portulacastrum), sometimes called sea purslane, or "ice plant," is a low-crawling ground cover. 'Akulikuli is an indigenous coastal ground cover found on all Hawaiian Islands and other islands in the Pacific. There's lots of it at Makalawena. Wetland and migratory birds like to forage through 'akulikuli looking for small invertebrates to eat. 'Akulikuli forms a dense mat and its leaves look like they are ready to pop because they are so succulent.

Winter can generate some great surfing waves at Makalawena. The best for board surfing is offshore the ironwood grove at the north end of the beach. *Warning, this is for seasoned surfers.*

The northernmost cove is good for snorkeling and looking at underwater formations. The middle cove, the large one below Pu'uali'i sand dune, the tallest dune, is best for body boarding, swimming long distances, floating on your back or on inflatables. The cove just south of Pu'uali'i, separated by the rocks jutting into the water, is probably best for snorkeling. The rocks are fun to explore, both above water and below. If you climb on top of them, you will find a little tide pool where the water has been warmed by the sun; it's just large enough for two to lie down in and not be seen by anyone on the beach; it's called the Lover's Pool. Guess why! But if you're not into making love, you can just luxuriate in total comfort while watching the little snails that inhabit the pool. They have an interesting life of their own.

When waves are really up, these rocks offer a good place from which to watch them; they crash up and over the rock and you get a REALLY CLOSE view of them, but you are quite protected. *If you are a good swimmer*, you can snorkel beneath these rocks; there is a sort of rocky tunnel connecting the two beaches that is interesting to explore.

It is at the edge of this beach also, close to the rocks, where I have frequently seen manta rays mating, an extraordinary sight. They come in close to shore usually around sunset.

Being immersed in the pristine elements of sunlight, pure air, sand and water is a spiritual experience, and at Makalawena, you can still have this experience. It's as if, since the beach is still rather difficult to get to, it hasn't been polluted by human beings' thought waves. One's mind and heart are washed clean here. The heart is uplifted, and the mind is stilled.

How lovely!

So now the promised personal experience.

I love to watch sunsets. Once, I just happened (how fortunate I was!) to be at Makalawena during the time of exact full moon, which occurred that day at approximately at 6:30 p.m. It was the end of the day. It had been beautiful and I had much to be thankful for.

I walked barefooted slowly along the shore. My footprints in the sands disappeared behind me like magic almost before I lifted my toes. The ancient, delicious smell of salt and old seashells, tangled algae and sunken treasure was in the air. As the sun began to go down, I climbed to the top of Pu'uali'i to watch.

The sun was throwing long columns of burnished gold across the water. The dazzling golden orb seemed to spin round and round, first in one direction, then the other, shooting out scintillating rays of white light that was hypnotic. Then steams of golden light like fire drenched the incoming foam of the waves in every hue of yellow and red—from amber, vanilla and lime to pinkish-rose to electric crimson to royal scarlet. The incoming waves made the sea into a giant kaleidoscope. I was mesmerized by the iridescent waves, like liquid carnival glass, rolling in one after another, disappearing into the sands as if into a magic mirror, leaving golden foam and silver crystal bubbles in their wake.

The sun now turned into a fiery orange ball, and a lone sailboat moved across it—her white sails were painted gold by the rays of the sun, and the craft itself became a black silhouette, passing in and then out of the orb of fire.

The sun then appeared again as a golden ball of light, dipping below the horizon, a vanishing starship—slowly, slowly, melting away into the distance. I watched until it became only a tiny white speck—then even tinier—then it was gone. But then to my astonishment, a green ray of light, like an arrow, shot directly out of the spot from where the sun had vanished; as quickly as it had flashed, it was gone. It was the famous phenomenon called "green flash."

But the flaming sky only became more inflamed. The clouds, the water, the beach seemed to be on fire!

For some reason, I turned and looked behind me, toward the volcanoes.

The larges, whitest moon in my life was just creeping up over the horizon!

The moon and sun were in a line, with me sitting on top of Pu'uali'i, in between. It was as though I was the fulcrum of a seesaw, and the moon and sun were sitting on either end of the seesaw.

In this direction, toward Mauna Kea and Hualalai volcanoes, the sky was painted every color of blue and silver and gray and lavender. The mountains themselves were deep lavender, with creases of deep purple and black. The sky was arranged in definite blocks of color, like those strips of sample color of paints—periwinkle and cerulean, cornflower, and Prussian blue, fading on one end into midnight blue. A halo of luminescent silver ringed the huge globe of the moon, which rose in what seemed like jerky movements, as if it were being pulled up by invisible strings, like a puppet. Distinct white beams shot out over the landscape in every direction.

I had the strange feeling that all this was for my benefit alone.

I was being blessed.

God bless this enchanted world, I cried from my heart.

The whole earth is my temple. I adore you!

I thought about those lines of Yeats that I had memorized so many years ago because I had thought them so beautiful. Only now, so many years later, I truly understood them.

"We must laugh, and we must sing. We are blessed by everything. Everything we look upon is blessed."

I felt happy, ecstatic. What a beautiful, blessed world!

So...perhaps…if you time it just right during a full moon at Makalawena, if you sit on top of Pu'uali'i as the sun begins to set… if you are favored by the gods and goddesses…you too can have a similar experience.

I hope you do!

Please remember, if you park at Mahai'ula, the gate closes at 7 p.m. (Second and last warning!) You probably don't have enough time to experience sunset at Makalawena and get back over the trail and along the beach before closing, so if you want to experience sunset and moon rise, either drive into Makalawena, or hike in from the highway.

Or fly in on a copter.

#2
Mahai'ula
(and Ka'elehuluhulu)

Getting there: *See the map above for Kekaha. Take Highway 19 from Kona. Drive 2.6 miles north of Kcahole Airport. Look for the **Kekaha Kai State Park** sign between the **mile-markers 90 and 91**. The 1.5-mile road to the sea, carved out of the treacherous a'a lava, is rough but doable in most vehicles.

Important note: the park is open between 9 a.m. and 7 p.m. but it is closed on Wednesdays. The gate is locked otherwise so take this seriously.

There is no fee. Amenities include picnic tables and portable toilets, but no water. Lots of shade from the palm trees.

There are actually two beaches here. The northernmost and loveliest beach here is Mahai'ula and the smaller, more southerly, one is Ka'elehuluhulu Beach, with its rocky, salt-and-pepper colored sand.

Ka'elehuluhulu, sometimes called "Second Beach," is frequented by pole and throw net fisherman. Great for colorful photos! If you look you will find a wide sandy opening in the rocks that provides entry and exit to good swimming and snorkeling offshore. There is an old wooden Hawaiian-style structure on the property as well as brackish ponds and plenty of shade.

Mahai'ula Beach itself is a perfectly crescent–shaped beach bordered by swaying palm trees and kiawe (mesquite, ouch!) The bay is well protected; the ocean bottom slopes gently away with patches of sand and rock. You'll find great swimming and snorkeling here. At the far north end of the beach is Kawili Point, a popular surf break; in fact, it has been regarded as one of the best surf spots since ancient times.

Mahai'ula was once a thriving fishing village. In fact, the name means "a place where fishermen dwell." Among other archeological sites in this area, including several old stone platforms and rock walls, is the wonderful Pohaku o Lama, the deity stone standing almost at the water's edge. During the spring, when algae bloom and the bay turns reddish-brown, it was believed that the stone goddess Pohaku o Lama was menstruating. The bay is still an important nursery for fish like pua and mullet.

In the 1930's, A. K. Magoon, a part-Hawaiian businessman, bought the property, which was by then all but deserted. The Magoon family house, called the "Magoon Mansion," is still located at the far north end of the beach. For years, the extended Magoon family visited the family home, especially in August, when the family celebrated the patriarch's birthday for days on end. Helen Desha Beamer, a renowned Hawaiian singer and composer, was often a guest, and she wrote a beautiful song celebrating this remarkable place.

Beautiful, really beautiful,
Mahai'ula in the calm,
Spread out into the distance,
And the shore break draws
Lacy pictures in the sands.

After the death of Magoon, the home became the Kona Diving Lodge for three years. Now, it is sadly empty, but if you climb the stairs and sit nearby, you might hear the silent happy echoes of long ago beach parties—the happy strumming of the ukulele, the laughter of children, the poignant singing voices, the sizzling of the luau.

Mahai'ula is a great place for scuba diving. Beyond the bay you will find "the Arches," with its many underwater arches, tunnels, and caves, and even two sunken ships. You will need to swim out past the lighter-colored water with the sandy bottom. Look for the dark colored water with the coral reef below, and snorkel to the north. You will likely see a thriving multi-colored reef with sea arches and caves.

On March 19, 1917, the Maui was carrying a full load of 13,360 bags of sugar from Kohala Plantation en route to Kailua-Kona when she encountered a severe local storm and ran aground. Her remains still lie offshore in water about 25 feet deep on rolling hills of pahoehoe lava. The engine, boiler, and parts of the hull structure still survive.

The Fuji Maru, a Japanese sampan, a tuna fishing boat, was enlisted as a patrol vessel to defend Hawaiian waters after the bombing at Pearl Harbor. She grounded while on patrol on January 12, 1943. Parts of her debris are in the bay and some parts are up in the trees above the beach. If you look closely at low tide, her engine can be seen in one of the sand channels directly off the beach at Ka'elehuluhulu. Close inshore are several tanks and assorted metal debris.

Mahai'ula is a great family beach (and *not* clothing optional), but keep an eye on children during high surf, usually in the winter months. During the more customary placid days, you may see the green sea turtle basking in the sand at the water's edge. In the evening, during dusk, the lights from the planes landing at the airport appear like magical stars and have a mesmerizing effect, but remember, check out time is 7 p.m. and the gate will be locked.

No camping, but if you backpack in from the highway, you *probably* won't be disturbed.

#3
Kua Bay
(Manini'owali Beach)

Getting there: *See the map above for Kekaha. Look for the access road just north of the 88 mile-marker. Kua Bay road is closer to the **89 mile-marker** and directly across from the entrance of the Veterans' Cemetery. It's a road just north of the Pu'u Ku'ili cinder cone, which rises prominently out of the flat lava landscape. **You cannot miss the cinder cone**. Drive in approximately one-fourth mile to the beach. The road is now paved (too, too bad! That means more people.) and there are new restroom with showers. Kua Bay is part of the Kekaha Kai State Park. That means on Wednesdays the Park is closed. It opens at 9 a.m. and closes at 7 p.m. all other days of the week. Remember that although the Park is closed and the gate is locked on Wednesdays, you can still hike in, although it's about a mile. Actually, this is a great day to go, since fewer people will be there. There is no lifeguard but may be soon. The paved road to this beach, the parking lot, and the permanent showers and restrooms are relatively recent "improvements," courtesy of the nearby luxury development of 2005. Before that, you had to park just off the highway and walk down a rough dirt road to this beach, but you got to have it pretty much to yourself, or maybe share it with a handful of surfers. The "improvements" have made it so easily accessible that now crowds of people are here on the weekend. For more private swimming and tanning, go on weekdays. Park facilities include parking, picnic tables, restrooms and water.

Kua Bay is also known as Manini'owali. A lovely gem, though small, once tucked away secretly in the basalt and African grass, Kua Bay is Kona's newest beach park (too bad!). Powdery white sand, turquoise water, a gentle slope—Kua Bay has it all, including some of the best swimming and boogie boarding on the island. There is virtually no shade, so be prepared; the sun can be scorching but swimming and boogie boarding in the crystal waters is primo, and cliff-jumping from the rocks offshore can be great fun. Snorkeling the clear, turquoise waters along the rocks to the north is excellent unless the surf or wind picks up. **Show great respect for the strong currents and large waves here; if surf is up, don't go in.** Kua Bay is best enjoyed in the mornings, before strong winds pick up as happens often in the afternoons.

In winter, sand is sometimes shifted offshore, and the beach becomes rocky. Also, **watch out for rip currents and high surf that breaks over the large rocks.** Only experienced bodysurfers should ride these kinds of waves.

Manini'owali gets its name from a romantic legend of three people who were involved in a love triangle. They were turned to stone by the powerful kahuna, Kikaua. The three unfortunates were Manini'owali, a princess from Manini'owali; Uluweuweu, the man Manini'owali was engaged to; and Kahawaliwali, the chiefess with whom Uluweuweu fell in love. The stone formation that stands at Kikaua Point Beach (near mile-marker 87 on Route 19) is said to be Kahawaliwali. The stone formation has a two-legged base and is one of the most prominent shoreline landmarks at Kikaua Point.

There are sacred, native Hawaiian sites and ruins to the north of the beach; please do not disturb them.

Just north of the beach is a stand of palm trees and a freshwater spring. The spring looks so inviting; however, the bottom of the pool is not sand but rotting palm fronds. Don't jump in; you'll be sorry. You'll be coated with the rotting, stinky mess.

A short hike from the access road takes one to the peak of Pu'u Ku'ili, the 342-foot high cinder cone mentioned previously. This is a great spot from which to watch sunsets and whales, and it has a majestic view of the Kohala coastline.

There is also the wonderful hike along the shoreline Ala Ali'i Trail (Way of the Kings) to Makalawena Beach, just to the south. The hike takes about an hour and a half; you probably need water. About halfway along this hike is a little cove where backpackers might *discreetly* camp. Wild goats are frequently seen in this area, as are dolphins, turtles and whales in season.

I hope you enjoy this magnificent stretch of coast including Kekaha Kai State Park and Makalawena. Now for something completely different.

#4
Napo'opo'o Beach at Kealakekua Bay

How to get there: To get there you head south from Kailua-Kona on Highway 11. Between the **111 and the 110 mile-markers**, at a Y in the road, you will see the small Napo'opo'o Road sign. Look sharp —the sign is small and comes up fast. Turn right and wind down, down, down until you come to a fork.

There are still some of the famous old coffee shacks standing; you may, if you watch closely, see a couple of them as you head down the road. Not too many are left, but back in the day, you could rent one for fifty dollars a month. The rustic life was the good life!

Keep going down, down, down. There's really no other way you can go. It's a lovely, scenic drive about four miles to the sea. There are more than 100 curves to the beach; I've counted them! Notice how the terrain quickly changes. It gets drier and drier, as you near the beach, until it's quite arid.

You can either park at the old wharf at the bottom of the road, right beyond the stop sign, or you can turn right at the wharf and park at the end of the road, at the Kealakekua Beach Park.

Facilities include restrooms, picnic pavilion, trashcans, drinking water, and showers.

See the map on the following page.

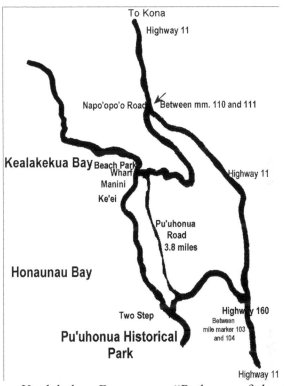

Kealakekua Bay means "Pathway of the God Bay." My old stomping grounds! I've driven the more than 100 curves down to this beach *countless* times. For years I swam the one-mile across the bay to the Cook Monument and back several days a week. I almost died at this beach twice. It has a lot of personal history for me. For the ancient Hawaiians, it was also one of the most beloved and historical places of all the Islands. For western historians too, this beach has huge significance. This bay is the second most important historical site in the Hawaiian Islands, at least from the western point of view, second only to Ka Lae, commonly called South Point, where the first Hawaiians are believed to have first landed. A *lot* happened here at Kealakekua!

For one thing, this is where the famed Captain James Cook, who discovered the Islands for the western world in 1778, died. Captain Cook was initially revered as the god Lono, some historians say, though others dispute this, when he sailed into the bay, but in any case all homage was paid to him and his men. The bounty of the island was heaped upon him, and it is said that 50,000 people crowded into the bay to worship him, or just have a look. After a month's stay in the bay, his ships departed, but due to a broken foremast, returned to the bay. The islanders, having wined and dined him and his crew at great expense for a month (so to speak, the natives didn't have wine, but they did have 'awa, a euphoriant and relaxant), were none too happy to see him return.

History is nebulous on exactly what happened, but it seems that once the islanders realized that Cook was not a god, or any rate was vulnerable like all men, he was killed in an altercation over a stolen boat. The exact site was at Ka'awaloa, a small village on the northern side of the bay. There is a 27-foot white obelisk erected near the spot, easily seen from almost anywhere in the bay. The land around the obelisk was bought by the British consul general in Hawaii in 1877 for one dollar! Since then it has been maintained by the Royal Navy, as well as by a caretaker paid by the British embassy in Washington. There is some doubt over whether the monument strictly belongs to the British government or the descendants of the consul who bought it.

Kealakekua Bay, encompassing 315 acres, and 1.5 miles long and one mile wide, is a State Historical Park; actually, this State Historical Park is underwater. It is a designated Marine Life Conservation District, and is the largest natural sheltered bay of the Island. The State of Hawaii has declared the entire Kealakekua Bay as a State Marine Sanctuary.

This bay is the number one destination for the snorkeling cruises on the Big Island for good reason. The pristine color of the water and the variety of marine life are outstanding. Erosive rainwater runs off away from the bay, keeping mud and silt out. There are strict rules for construction above the bay to insure the current drainage pattern. The deep green water here is crystal clear and abundant with living coral reefs and many varieties of marine life, with water visibility to 100 feet. This is one of the very best snorkeling and diving sites on the Big Island, with its calm, protected waters and sunny skies most days of the year.

Kealakekua Bay is the most famous of all Hawaii beaches for its spinner dolphins. Almost every early morning, that is, before 10 a.m. but sometimes later, these delightful creatures sport about in the sunshine with happy abandon. If you are really fortunate you can swim with them, though disturbing them in any way—chasing after them, trying to touch them, etc.—is strictly illegal. However, the truth is, these dolphins seem to *enjoy* people; they certainly don't swim away unless they are really harassed. I myself have had the enduring thrill of swimming about in the bay or kayaking and suddenly, to my great happiness, being completely surrounded by these cavorting, joyful creatures. Their happiness and merriment is contagious. If you are underwater with them, you can hear a strange, high-pitched squealing sound; they are singing to one another.

The primary beach of Napo'opo'o, fronting the park, is a narrow strip of sand fronting a fairly wide strip of boulders, large and small. You have to walk gingerly over these boulders to get into the water. Wave action rocks these boulders to and fro, creating a wonderful lilting music—be careful, though, or you can get your ankles bruised rather severely when entering or exiting the water.

There almost always is wave action here, good for body surfing and boogie boarding, not for board surfing. In high surf, be very careful. Though once you get out there, the water may be calm and placid, getting in and out can be tricky. This beach was the second beach I ever visited when I was a newbie to the Island, and I almost drowned here. When I tried to exit the water, a huge wave pounded me to the floor bottom of the sea and held me down. Luckily I could hold my breath for a fairly long time.

Another time I saw a really comical sight here. Keep in mind that this is a beach community; quite a few locals spend their mornings lolling about on the sand, just watching the surf. It's more common than not that the continuous wave action near the boulders lifts the water very high, and then lowers it down again. Once, I happened to be there when a tourist couple jauntily made their way into the water; the gal was dressed in a designer bikini. She got out into the calmer waters fairly easily, but when she tried to come back ashore, a huge wave first pulled her underwater, then lifted her straight up, high, high, high into the air, as if for everyone on the beach to see. I'll never forget the look on that gal's face, as she was hoisted up minus her bikini top. Everyone got an eyeful.

There is some great snorkeling out among the rocks just to the left of the bay, as you face the sea. They are almost directly in front of the stonewall. You'll see schools of various fish here.

It was about 300 feet out from the rocks here that I had one of the biggest, at first scariest, and finally best, surprises of my life. It was in 1999. I was kayaking alone one early morning; I had started from the opposite side of the beach, and I was hoping to find the dolphins. I had just put my paddle aside and was sitting quietly, staring into the water, when suddenly my kayak began to rock. To my astonishment and horror, a barnacle-encrusted behemoth began to rise out of the water directly beside me, less than six feet away. I remember thinking that I must be having a nightmare. One giant eye, the size of a large grapefruit, stared directly at me, sizing me up it seemed, for a very long moment. I was stunned to hear what sounded like someone on a ventilator. I was too surprised to scream. Then the creature slowly rose higher out of the water, and as she did, my kayak rocked violently, so that I hung on to the sides until my knuckles were white; I was afraid I was going to be pitched into the water. Then the creature, satisfied with her estimation of me, slowly sank back down into the water.

It was a humpback whale!

It was a very rare occasion that a humpback whale was swimming in the bay with her calf. Later, I found out that her baby had been born in the bay. Highly unusual! She stayed in the bay a few weeks; people who lived in the bay said they could hear her and her baby slapping their tails through the night.

Just in back of the sand, you'll see the Hikiau Heiau, an ancient Hawaiian temple site that was built by King Kalani'opu'u. This heiau was dedicated to the god Lono, and the prophecy was that someday he would return to this very bay. When Captain Cook sailed into the bay at the very time of Makahiki, the celebration time of Lono, his ships were resplendent with the symbol of Lono, a symbol that looked like a square sail. No wonder he might have been mistaken for the god.

Originally, the heiau was more than 100 feet wide and 250 long. It was a *luakini* heiau; that is, it was used for human sacrifice. The small stone platform at the top is believed to have been the altar. It was in this heiau that Captain Cook was, according to some historians, deified. However, the respect doesn't seem to have been mutual; Cook's men, to the horror of the Hawaiians, blatantly disassembled the wooden temple for their firewood! This is also said to be the site of the first Christian service in Hawaii; Captain Cook performed a funeral service here for one of his men.

Look toward the north at the sheer cliffs, called Pali-kapu-o-Keoua. The name means "forbidden cliffs of Keoua," in honor of Keoua Nui, known as the "father of kings," since many subsequent kings were his descendants. The difficulty in accessing the cliffs kept the exact burial places secret. On the cliff's face numerous lava tube openings are visible, many of which are ancient Hawaiian burial caves. You can't climb these cliffs, but you can snorkel around the edges. The waters here are good for snorkeling during calm water conditions. Abundant coral growth and marine life can be seen in waters of about five feet.

In the northern part of the bay, beyond the cliffs, where the Captain Cook monument stands, is one of the most sheltered anchorages on the coast, even during high surf and Kona storms. The bay's best diving is said to be here at Ka'awaloa Cove, where water depth ranges from about 5 to 120 feet. You'll find a huge variety of fish here. The Humuhumunukunukuapua'a, Hawaii's state fish, as well as the brilliant, multi-colored parrotfish, yellow tang, the orange spine unicorn fish, the ornate butterfly fish, the yellow trumpet fish, the surgeon, the peacock grouper, the Black Triggerfish, the blue fin Jack Trevally, and many, many more, swim nonchalantly about the technicolor reefs.

The bottom is deep here, and attracts many commercial diving tours. If you are a good swimmer, you can swim here from other points of the bay. You can also kayak. If you don't have your own kayak, I recommend Kona Boys, which is located in Kealakekua, on the way from Kona to Kealakekua Bay. They give kayak tours. Their number is 328-1234. Take a photo of their establishment with the cute sign that reads, "Love your mother." There are no kayak rentals at the bay.

There are several snorkeling and glass bottom boat cruises to Kealakekua Bay, which are extremely popular. Captain Zodiac (808-329-3199) and the Fair Wind ((800-322-2788) have been around forever.

You can also get into the water at the old wharf. There are steps leading down that can't be seen from above. Try snorkeling to the right, near the shore.

Keep in mind, *he, he*, that this bay is said to have the greatest density of hammerhead sharks of any place on the planet! There is also a resident reef shark that has been there for years, at least twenty. He lives, or at least sleeps, near the old wharf. I've never seen the seven-foot plus fellow, never wanted to, but a lot of my friends have. One guy I know says he goes down fairly regularly during day hours and touches his sleeping nose!

Well, I've told you where to look! Up to you if you want to pet him.

If it eases your mind, in case you are not specifically looking for sharks, in all my days of swimming in the bay, I have only seen one, and it was a little baby, about three feet long. I have seen some pretty fierce-looking BIG barracudas, however, and some large manta rays.

#5
Manini Beach

Getting there: *Follow the directions above to Kealakekua Bay. Beginning at the very bottom of Napo'opo'o Road, turn left at the landing and then take the first right onto narrow Manini Beach Road. Go straight ahead about a half block until you see the green sign that that says, "This special and sacred environment has been known since earliest time as Kapahukapu." The entrance is usually chained.

If you can't get a parking spot, just park in the lot at the bottom of Napo'opo'o Road and walk over in five minutes.

Sweet little Manini beach is my favorite spot on Kealakekua Bay, and do I have so many wonderful memories of this idyllic place. It *was* tucked quietly behind a very large, multi-million dollar two-story beach house, which made a good landmark, and also kept it more hidden and more private, but Manini Beach and the entire Napo'opo'o beach area were hit hard on March 11, 2011, when the Japanese 9.0 tsunami Japan washed ashore here and caused extensive damage. The big blue house, which I had often enjoyed with my friends, was washed whole into the bay.

The sign welcomes visitors who will respect and preserve the land, and asks that certain rules be abided by in protecting its ecosystem, such as: no launching of kayaks and no vehicles on the beach, also no camping. However, if you are respectful, you might take your sleeping bag ONLY and sleep out under the stars.

Look seaward just a few steps into the park for the small but noticeable patch of sizeable white coral and black rock that leads to a small clear sand channel in the water, allowing access out to the coastal reef and deep bay waters. You'll see a *very* small patch of sand. This is the safe entrance into the bay. Just snorkel between the rocks and you're out! From here, it's a great swim to Napo'opo'o Beach, or over to the point, which is one mile across. Keep in mind that sharks come into the bay in the evening to feed.

He he!

The grassy area is great for sunbathing and picnicking. There is lots of shade, but no other amenities.

The area between the Napo'opo'o landing and the southern tip of Manini Beach Point is the most interesting for scuba diving or snorkeling, where encrusted coral, caves, crevices and ledges can be found. Sometimes surfing is good on the mauka side of the point; make sure the waves break far enough out so that the rocks are avoided.

Hiking around the Point is also interesting. You probably need slippers. Manini is a great place to watch the sunsets, and also a good vantage point during storms. Of course, not *too* big of storms!

You can get a real flavor of the easy-going, carefree local life here at Napo'opo'o Village. The *kane* stroll around barefooted in cutoffs, the *wahines* saunter about draped gracefully in colorful pareos. Donkeys, dogs and cats wander about where ever they want. Small children, already accomplished in reading the various moods of the sea, dive off the rocks. It seems nobody ever has to go *to work*! What a life!

Many of the old Hawaiian families with roots here still live here. The famous hula dancer Iolani Luakini was born here and lived here in the later part of her life. The renowned healer and teacher, Auntie Margaret Machado, lived and taught right here in her beach house until her recent death. Auntie Margaret was the epitome of aloha and honored as a Hawaiian Living Treasure; she taught thousands of students from around the globe her sacred gift, *lomilomi*, the

Hawaiian way of healing. She was an incredibly beautiful person; I wept the first time I met her.

Back in the seventies and eighties, the Bay was where a lot of the transplanted hippies hung out. Back then, a day wasn't a day until you had hung out at the Bay. Back then, a morning was a morning—an almost endless stretch of time when you could stretch out on the sand and warm your bones, listen to the song of the rocks rolling up and down the beach, chat idly with your friends while you drank fresh coconut water and ate spoon meat, swim over to the monument, take a leisurely walk down the road to see who was doing what...

Ah, how time flies!

#6
Ke'ei Beach

Getting there: Ke'ei is just south of Kealakekua Bay. Coming from the bottom of Napo'opo'o at the wharf (see the map for Kealakekua Bay) you can reach Ke'ei village by turning left onto Pu'uhonua Road, which connects Kealakekua Bay and Place of Refuge. Drive on a half-mile to open lava fields; you will pass Keawaiki Road—if you reach the transfer station (a transfer station is a garbage dump), you have gone too far. Take the next right after Keawaiki, which is Ke'ei Road (maybe no sign!). The road is rough to say the least but if drive carefully, you can do it in a compact. It's less than a half *very rough* mile to a parking area. The road gets, let's say, bumpier, as you go.

If you drive in, note the stone wall—just beyond the larger parking area you can walk further along the road, in between the homes, which consist of newer houses and the fabled "coffee shacks."

Park on the right across from the first house, ***making sure not to block the driveways***. Some of the residents here are very territorial. **Be *very* polite, respectful, and quiet.** Otherwise, you are very likely to experience the exact opposite of "aloha." Walk further along the road, in between the houses and lines of coconut trees, over a patch of black lava rocks to a large stone wall and stone walk-way. Around the corner of the wall, Ke'ei Beach becomes visible in its entirety as a black and white speckled sandy beach, thin and hilly, but with shade—perfect for relaxing. From here, if you wish, you can also hike south to Palemano Point. Ke'ei Village to Palemano Point is 1.5 miles.

Be sure and take water, sunscreen, slippers, etc. No amenities. No lifeguard.

You can also hike to Ke'ei from the south side of Kealakekua Bay, to Palemano Point, which I highly recommend. Not only do you avoid offending the locals with parking problems—it's an unforgettable hike over white coral, which always reminds me of walking on bleached bones, which, of course, it really is—the bones of coral. Begin at the Napo'opo'o Village road. You will be walking between lava walls and palm trees. Then walk along the seawall that will take you straight to Ke'ei beach. It's about 1.3 miles. Palemano Point is beyond the beach, on the low, pahoehoe lava fields. One of

Ke'ei's attractions is the grotto on the smooth lava bluff at the water's edge near the parking area. Waves wash into three, land-locked caverns formed by large collapsed lava tubes.

I love Ke'ei. It's old Hawaii. It's a local beach, one that few tourists visit. The old fishing village of Ke'ei is one of those places where time seems almost to stand still. A day there just lingers on and on. Old outrigger canoes sit amidst ruins of houses long gone. Dogs lay around doing their thing. The sun is hot. The breezes are cool. Green palm trees sway against the blue sky.

Ke'ei is also one of the most important historical sites in Hawaii, and besides that, there is a fascinating tale of shipwreck at this picturesque beach. For divers, this is one of the very best spots on the Big Island to dive.

First, the history. The battle of Moku'ohai (alternative spelling: Moku'akae) was fought here in 1782 and was a key battle in the early days of Kamehameha's wars to conquer all of the Hawaiian Islands. It was his first major victory, solidifying his leadership over much of the island. This bay, now called Moku'akae (which could be a misspelling of Moku'ohai), is just south of Palemano point. The name means "grove of 'ohai trees" for the *Sesbania tomentosa*, which is now endangered, and no longer exists in the area but once might have been plentiful. It was during this battle that the renowned red feather cloak of Kiwala'o, now in the Bishop Museum, was captured by Kamehameha the Great. Feathered cloaks were sort of the equivalent of gold crowns to the Hawaiians; they were symbols of royalty and prestige.

Kame'eiamoku, one of Kamehameha's men, was the first chief injured, but when Kiwala'o, the enemy, wearing the famed red-feathered cloak, approached to finish him off, another of Kamehameha's men came to his aid. Kiwala'o was hit by a sling stone, and the injured Kame'eiamoku crawled over to him and slit his throat with a sharks-tooth dagger. Many men died in this battle, and it was said that the women and children from both camps flooded into the nearby "place of refuge," which we will read about later.

Once you know the story, it's impossible to spend the day at Ke'ei without being aware of the great amount of blood that was shed here.

Now for the fascinating tale of shipwreck.

Englishman Thomas Cavendish is credited for having been the first intentionally to circumnavigate the globe from 1586-88. There were others before him, but they apparently had no idea what they were doing. Cavendish was a Member of Parliament, and sailed to Virginia in 1585. He is regarded by some historians as a pirate of infamy who committed rape and murder, and plundered the riches of the New World with impunity, rather than as a British pillar of virtue.

On November 14, 1587, Cavendish, commanding the 120-ton Desire and the 60-ton Content, attacked the 700-ton Spanish galleon Santa Anna at sea. The battle raged for five to six hours before the Spanish captain surrendered. Cavendish's men took the Santa Anna into port at Cape St. Lucas. The galleon was despoiled of her treasures—highly prized satins, silks, damasks, wines, and musk, and also 122,000 pieces of gold and silver pesos, and another 1.2 million in gold, an immense treasure.

Not all the treasure from the Santa Anna could be stowed on the English vessels, as they were too small for all the booty. The remainder of the treasure was still in the ship's hold when the galleon was burned in port on November 17th. Cavendish stranded the galleon's crew and passengers, about 190 people, as well. After firing a parting ironic salute to the deserted Spaniards, the Desire and the Content sailed away. Coming out of the bay, however, the Content, commanded by Steven Hare, lagged behind and was never seen again. Karma, perhaps?

There are, however, two accounts, based on native legend, that claim the ship was wrecked, at two separate locations. One account claims the Content wrecked in a sheltered bay north of Cabo San Lucas, but the second account comes from Hawaiian natives who say a pirate ship named Content sank on the reefs of Palemano Point off the island of Hawaii. Off Ke'ei, to be exact. The Content and her prized treasure have never been found.

To my mind, there is even a more fascinating legend. This one also involves shipwreck. In 1527, three Spanish ships led by Cortez sailed from Mexico, for the Molucca Islands. Only one reached its destination, for a fierce storm drove the little company far north of the usual route, and swept two of the ships into the unknown. There are accounts that a foreign vessel was wrecked about this time on the Kona coast of Hawaii, and must have been one of these missing ships. A white man and woman swam ashore. After reaching the beach, they knelt for a long time in prayer. The islanders, watching them, waited until they rose, and then welcomed them. The place was named "Kulou," which means "kneeling." The Hawaiians received their white visitors as guests, and they married into the ali'i caste. In the Hawaiian legends, the man and woman are called brother and sister. The man was named Kukanaloa. Their descendants became well known, one of them becoming a governor of the island of Kauai. These white citizens came to the islands in the reign of Kealiiokaloa, who became a king of Hawaii about 1525.

Interestingly, it was said that the first westerners in the Islands encountered natives with blue eyes. This lends credence to this legend. Just for the record, if you're into reincarnation theory, I have a friend here who claims that she and her brother were just that brother and sister of this legend.

Ke'ei Beach is a gem. I'm glad some guidebooks barely mention it, or, even better, don't mention it at all! It's ideal for those who want to spend a lackadaisical day sunbathing among the beautiful coconut trees and the beautiful view of Kealakekua Bay. There are a few picnic tables, and the locals have built a small pool for the *keikis*, the kids. It is also *at times* very good for surfing and body boarding, and it is excellent for snorkeling and scuba diving, for *experienced* snorkelers and divers, *not so much for children.* The sand is a coarse salt and pepper sand, good for running and playing and Frisbee. There is a narrow sandy channel at the northern end of the beach that's suitable for swimming. The reef stretches offshore for almost 300 yards. Keep in mind, however, that this is a remote beach, as far as quick access, with open exposure to the sea, and with no lifeguards. **Children should be watched carefully.**

The ocean bottom is fairly rocky, but surfers have cleared a path to get out to the breaks; the entry is just inside the small stonewall where it is shallow and there is a small strip of sand. At any rate, it is advisable to only enter the water at the break points, long or wide strips of sand where there is no coral visible under the water—you can spot them as the brightness of the water stands out among the dark coral coloring. From the stonewall here you may swim out to deeper waters; the ground drops quickly away. Some people choose to start and end their kayak trips across the bay from here.

The sea coves at Ke'ei offer some of the best snorkeling of the island. Marine life is fantastic; you'll see lots of eels. In fact, at the 80-90 feet level, you'll find the "Garden of Eels." Then work your way up to the reef. There is plenty to see in the 20-30 ft depth as well. Many varieties of coral are abundant and there are some great lava tubes and at least one very deep cavern, as well as many chimneys. Easiest entry is through the old canoe ramp, behind the little rock wall.

Night dives are exceptional.

This portion of the bay is primarily coral reef, the resting place of sea turtles and marine life. Occasionally, you might see a monk seal.

Palemano Point near Ke'ei beach literally means "shark defense." It is low and flat; you will see coconut trees and temple ruins near its outer end. The buildings of a resort camp on the point are prominent.

Here the reef is formed such that sharks cannot get into the area (I suppose there's always a first time?) Surfing at Palemano Point is unpredictable and you just have to be there to know the conditions. On the other hand, Palemano Point is an isolated spot where surfers aren't vying with one another for territory. On good days, there are some of the biggest waves and longest rides.

South of Palemano Point is a long narrow storm beach of sand of undeveloped shoreline which leads to Moku'ohai Bay. A mass of bare rocks extends 125 yards off the north side of the point. About a quarter-mile north of the point, an old lava flow reaches the shoreline. In winter, this is a good whale watching area.

#7
Pu'uhonua o Honaunau

Getting there: From Highway 11 turn onto Highway 160 at the Honaunau Post Office, **between mile-markers 103 and 104**. (It's approximately 20 miles from Kailua-Kona). You will be heading toward the ocean on a beautiful road that serpentines down to the sea (great fun on a bicycle, at least the going down!). After three-and-a-half miles you will see a turn off on the left for **Pu'uhonua o Honaunau National Historical Park**. You can't miss it. Entrance into the park is five dollars per vehicle, and is good for seven days. The sun is often really *hot* here; take lots of water. Also, this is a great place to picnic.

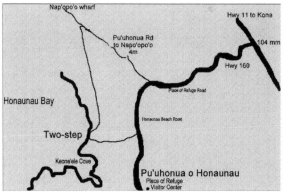

Pu'uhonua o Honaunau, called "Place of Refuge," and sometimes "City of Refuge" is a National Historical Park of 186 acres. What is a "Place of Refuge"?

In ancient times, each of the major islands had one or more sanctuaries, called *pu'uhonua*; the Big

Island had six, one in each of its districts. If a *kapu*, a law, were broken, the lawbreaker could escape death by reaching the sanctity of the nearest pu'uhonua. Some interesting kapus were such as eating a banana if you were a woman, stepping on a chief's shadow, or spilling the king's spit bowl. During times of war, old men, women and children could also seek safety in the pu'uhonua, as well as defeated warriors.

The ancient village of Honaunau was the ancestral home of the Kamehameha dynasty, serving in ancient times as a major Hawaiian religious and cultural center. When Kamehameha's great-grandfather died around 1650, his bones were placed in a temple here constructed on a platform next to the refuge. His mana, his spiritual energy inherited from his ancestral gods, and the mana of his descendants, became the power protecting the refuge at Honaunau. The Hale-o-Keawe, the royal mausoleum, held the bones of some of Kamehameha's ancestors as well as great warriors who excelled in their art and courage.

After King Kamehameha's death, with the overthrow of the kapu system and then the coming of the missionaries, Kamehameha's favorite and very powerful queen ordered that all of the sacred temples and idols be destroyed, with the exception of this one; possibly it was spared because it housed the bones of Kamehameha's ancestors. The bones of King Kamehameha himself were never housed here; his bones were hidden by retainers and have never been found, as he wished. It wasn't only that he dreaded the ultimate insult and sacrilege of his bones falling into the hands of enemies and being made into fishhooks or arrows for shooting rats; it was the belief that the mana of his bones must go back into the earth, to protect future generations of his people. For the sad tale of the rape and plunder of this temple by westerners, see the story "House of Bones" in *Bones of Love*, a thought-provoking collection of stories about ancient Hawaii (available at Amazon.com and Volcano Art Gallery).

Although ancient canoes moved easily in and out of the small harbor of Honaunau Bay, the water was not deep enough for the European and American trading ships that began arriving late in the eighteenth century. Kamehameha, who wished to stimulate social and economic interaction with the foreigners, moved his business, so to speak, to deeper harbors. Honaunau thus declined in importance, and with the abolition of the kapu system in 1819, absolution and forgiveness provided by places of refuge became obsolete.

Many visitors to Hawaii find the Place of Refuge, after Kilauea Volcano, to be the most fascinating place they visit. You can almost step back in time here, where ancient temples and *ki'i* (wooden images) have been reconstructed as authentically as possible. You can see here the pu'uhonua and a complex of archeological sites including temple platforms, royal fishponds, sledding tracks, burial cliffs, and some coastal village sites. The Park is very well maintained, and self-guided as well as ranger-guided tours are available. Cultural events, including authentic hula performances, take place—you can find out what events are happening by calling the Park at 808-328-2326. I suggest you call in advance of your visit; there are some wonderful programs here.

For a real treat, explore the backcountry trail, a two-mile round trip hike along the 1871 trail, where you will find ancient heiau (temples), holua sled courses, and the dramatic Keanae'e cliffs. This trail originally connected the coastal villages along the south Kona coast. There are burial caves all along the cliffs. You can get directions at the Park entrance.

The Keanae'e cliffs! How they are forever etched in my memory! When I first came to Hawaii thirty years ago, it was from these 45-feet high cliffs that I for the first time dove headfirst into Hawaiian waters. What was I thinking! I would never do it now, that's for sure! But at the time, in the company of two young bucks who nonchalantly dove in before me, I didn't think much about it; I hesitated just the briefest moment before plummeting in right behind them. We swam across the water to the cliffs on the other side, and only when we swam back and I looked up at the cliffs, which completely surrounded me on three sides, and then I looked at the open ocean with its huge waves surging in front of me, did I wonder how I was going to get *out* of the water.

But the two young bucks showed me how. All you had to do, they said, was wait for one of the great waves to lift you up high to the top of the cliff, and then you had to scurry to get your feet into a tiny foothold on the ledge just below the top of the cliff and then heave yourself up and over. Only drawback was that if your timing was not just right, you would be unable to get a foothold and handhold and then the wave surge would carry you to the adjacent cliff where you would be dashed against the rocks, probably instantly breaking every bone in your body.

The two bucks went first, showing me how, and then stood on the cliffs looking down and laughing at me. Having no choice, for there was no other way out of the water—I couldn't possibly swim out to the open ocean with its enormous waves—I did it, with beating heart. But having done it once, it was no fear. For years after that, I often jumped from those cliffs and swam the distance to the other side, without a thought of the sharks that must swim those waters.

Ah, youth!

However, thanks to progress (?), swimming and diving in the Park is no longer permitted. Someone finally *did* die jumping off those cliffs. Snorkelers and swimmers are forbidden now to enter the water at Keone'ele Cove within the Park. Too bad! Fishing is permitted, as well as picnicking; there are charcoal grills. There are also restroom facilities. But for some of the best snorkeling in Hawaiian waters, however, there is wonderful nearby Two-Step.

Just another note: I always love to go to Place of Refuge on stormy days, or when a storm is just gathering. The wind, the very high surf, the bending palm trees, the salty sea smell—it all just does something for my soul.

#8
Two-Step Beach
(Keone'ele Cove)

Getting there: *See the map above for Place of Refuge. From Highway 11 turn onto Highway 160 at the Honaunau Post Office, between **mile-markers 103 and 104**. (Approximately 20 miles from Kailua-Kona). You will be heading toward the ocean on the beautiful road that serpentines down to the sea. After three and a half miles you will see a turn off on the left for Pu'uhonua o Honaunau National Historical Park. Just before the park gate, on the right, is a one-lane road that snakes past Two-Step Beach. You can either park in the National Park lot for $5, which includes park admission, and also allows you to use the bathroom facilities, or along the road for free, if you're not visiting the park. Make sure to lock your car and keep any valuables with you; theft and vandalism do sometimes occur here. I would suggest parking at the Park.

You can also get here from Napo'opo'o Beach. At the Napo'opo'o wharf, turn left and follow the coastal road four miles. You will end up at the entrance to the Park.

Parking for Two Step Beach is along the shore under the trees, just beyond the boat ramp. If no parking is available here, go back and park in the National Historic Park lot.

Two-Step**,** on Honaunau Bay, just steps from the Park entrance, offers some of the finest protected snorkeling and scuba diving, some say, in the world, certainly in the State. Besides the multi-colored living coral and colorful tropical fish, you are likely to see turtles, and if you go early in the morning, you may have the great good fortune to see spinner dolphins. However, please note the sign: *Dolphin Rest Area*. This is the area where dolphins rest during the day; **federal law prohibits approaching within 150 feet of them.**

You enter the water by stepping off the short cliff into the water near the center edge of the lava bench. There are two ledges that serve as steps down into the ocean; that's why it's called Two-Step! At low tide, it's a simple matter of stepping down these steps. At high tide, you can just step off into the water.

To get out, simply float up to the steps and wait for an incoming wave to float you up onto the bottom step. **Do not** put your fingers into the small holes in the rocks to haul yourself out—those holes are the homes of grouchy spiny sea urchins. Ouch! Always lay your hands on the rocks palms down flat, don't use fingers.

You can also walk down the boat ramp. The water around the ramp is chilly because of nearby springs, but it gets warmer and clearer as you swim past the little point of rocks that separates Keone'ele Cove from Honaunau Bay.

The very best snorkeling is along the edges of the cliffs, and the shallow waters adjacent to the shore. This is where you will see the most fish. But in the deeper waters you will find magnificent coral gardens.

There may be lots of turtles—the turtles can be found off to the left of the bay, over by the refuge.

Like dolphins, they are federally protected. Do not approach them within 30 feet.

Be careful not to stray too far from shore; watch for currents and high surf—there are frequent drownings and near drownings here by people misjudging the surf.

There is a small, sandy beach next to the boat ramp that is great for the keikis. On the other side of the boat ramp, on the rocks near the shore entry, is a large tide pool with tiny fish and hermit crabs that is also good for the wee ones.

You can get a taste for local life here—the Honaunau Canoe club meets here, and Two-Step is popular with the local fisher folk, who, in general, love to talk story. You can make local friends here. Just know the word "brah-dah" or "brah," and don't act shocked or offended by the F-word, perhaps the most ubiquitous word in the Hawaiian language.

If you need ice, there is a house on the roadside that sells it—you'll see the sign.

I suggest a morning swim at Two-Step, and then a picnic lunch and exploration of Place of Refuge in the afternoon for a priceless day in Hawaii!

Now for my next beach, which means heading up north again!

#9
Beach 69 and Beach 67
(Wai'alea)

Don't laugh; this beach really is known to most residents as Beach 69, and not for the reason you might think! It's not a beach set aside for lovers, but it's romantic enough that it could be. Its Hawaiian name is Wai'alea, but it has been called Beach 69 for as long as there have been public utility poles. Public utility poles? Until recently, that was how it was found, by turning onto the dirt road at utility pole number 69! Both pole and the old parking lot are gone now, replaced by a new paved access road, parking lot and trail through the kiawe groves to the beach. There is also a smaller beach adjacent to it called Beach 67.

Getting there: From Kailua-Kona, head north and **just before mile-marker 70**, turn toward Puako on Puako Road. Before the road bends south toward the town of Puako, take the first right turn. Follow the road about a little more than a quarter of a mile. Wai'alea Bay Beach access road and parking will be on your second left. There are restrooms, picnic tables, water and showers available, but no lifeguards. There are also lots of bees, just to let you know. Also, just to let you know, if you do get stung by a bee, take a bit of the skin of a papaya and rub the inside skin on the sting. It will stop hurting immediately!

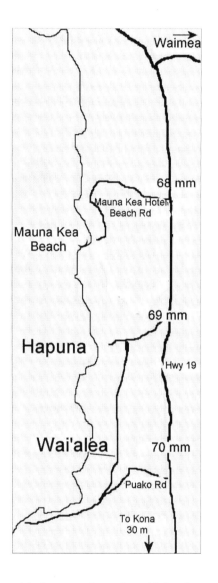

In the old days, only a handful of people knew about Beach 69. It was the kind of place you could go to and bump into your friends without planning on it; it was the kind of beach where you could swim and sunbathe in the nude without raising an eyebrow—you could camp here or even *live* here for a time. I used to camp here a lot. But times have changed. Many more people live on the Big Island, and many more visitors come here. But it's still a GREAT beach! And during the weekdays there still aren't a lot of people, but keep in mind that during high tide, there is very little beach in front of the trees—not a lot of room for a lot of people. Most of the trees are kiawe, mesquite trees—you know, those trees that drop the huge thorns all over the ground. Watch your step if you go barefoot, or wear slippahs!

Now officially called Wai'alea Bay Marine Preserve, Beach 69 is the larger of the two beaches on this bay. Both beaches have a secluded, rugged feel, and the bay is more protected and calmer than nearby Hapuna Beach, with its greater crowds. Private homes back up to the beach, but are barely visible. Please respect the private property, but you have access rights to the entire beach and bay.

In calm conditions, the bay has a soft sandy entry and great swimming, snorkeling, scuba diving and windsurfing; but during high surf, especially in the winter, ocean conditions can be hazardous, with rough water and strong currents.

From the end of the short trail turn right; this is a great spot for little children, with minimal surf and plenty of shade.

Most days, the water is gorgeously clear here until midmorning, when it becomes murkier. Even then, if you swim out a bit, you will find a chain of wee little islands leading northward to a long coral reef which makes fantastic snorkeling and diving. This beach is posted: no fishing by spear or net—this makes the fabulous fish less spooky and more approachable than at other sites. Creatures know when they are loved.

Behind the rock point in the middle of the bay is a small coral reef interesting to explore. Swim south towards the rock in the water that runs perpendicular to the beach; a little south of this rock you'll find a wonderfully diverse coral reef in seven to ten feet of water with lots of fish. Swim back and get out where you entered the water, or exit near the perpendicular rock and walk back down the beach.

If you are an experienced snorkeler and a strong swimmer, you might want to snorkel around the north cusp of Wai'alea, past the cove and the reef, past the sea arch and on to Hapuna Beach—a long distance swim, but one you will find remarkable, with underwater vistas to rival those of almost any place in the world. Please don't stand on the sea arch; it is crumbling.

Just walking the beach is a fascinating experience that inspires the imagination. The mangrove-like tree roots that extend above and below the sand furnish little niches for cozy privacy. Scattered driftwood and tree limbs and trunks in interesting shapes lie about and make for wonderful photos, if you are the artsy type.

At the far south end of the beach, before the sand meets a barricade of trees, there is a trail that veers to the left, up between the private homes. This trail is part of the Ala Kekaha Kai system that runs along the coast; it leads up to a private road and to a stretch of field, and down to the far end of Puako Bay.

To the north, there is a trail that leads to Beach 67, and then on to Hapuna Beach, about a mile away. Be mindful that the adjacent property to the trail is private property—be respectful.

Beach 67 is a small cove that is frequented by nudists and gay men. Sometimes there is some "activity" up on the bluffs in the trees and bushes and in the gullies just beyond the sandy area. Just to let you know.

Yes, Beach 69 brings back wonderful memories. I remember one time in particular, when I camped here with my lover. I remember waking at dawn, and marveling at how the dawning light coming from the cliffs above had turned the water to shimmering, iridescent golds and pinks. The morning star hung like a blue twinkling diamond over the glittering sea, while the gentle waves lapping against the shore seemed to whisper some timeless message to my soul. The dreamlike vision was made complete when a silent form, draped gracefully in a pareo, walked from the shadows of the trees to the waters edge, knelt in prayer, and then began playing a flute. The haunting, lilting melody, accompanied by the murmuring rhythm of the sea, seemed to awaken everything into existence—a single ray of white light burst from over the cliffs above, three golden dolphins somersaulted far into the sky, and a great, happy, twittering of birds arose from the trees.

Life was renewed.

#10
Hapuna
(The Springs of Life)

Getting there: No need map! (That's pigeon, for "You don't need a map.") If you're coming from Kona, or any of the hotels along the Kona coast, get on Highway 19 and head north. The turn off is well marked and is located just after Puako Beach Drive before mile-marker 69. Coming from Hilo, take Mamalahoa Highway into Waimea, and then turn onto Kawaihae Road. Stay on Kawaihae Road for ten miles and then turn left onto Highway 19. Head south for two miles, and the Hapuna turnoff will be on your right. The gate is open from 7:00 a.m. to 8:00 p.m. every day, and there is plenty of parking space. The beach and parking are free.

Oh, the golden mornings of chasing after a Frisbee, laughing and leaping and spinning and diving into the soft sand. The golden mornings of doing yoga at the edge of the water—stretching into downward dogs, headstands, backbends. The golden mornings of sprinting up and down the long, delicious stretch of beach, with the wind in my long hair and smell of salt spray in my lungs. The unforgettable, luscious smell of Coppertone sun-tanning lotion. The yummy taste of a sun-warmed tangerine for lunch. The cold outdoor shower, feeling the sand run through my bathing suit and down my legs and into the purple pohuehue blossoms that surround the shower. The ride back to Kailua in my Mustang convertible, with the top down, drying my long hair in the wind.

Hapuna is a beach for sensualists.

Back in the days, when I owned an art gallery in Kailua town, the highway was just a few years old, and there was hardly any traffic on it. In fact, sometimes you could drive all the way from Kailua to Hapuna or vice versa and not pass a single car! Gas was only thirty cents a gallon. Hard to believe now! But back then, it was just a quick 25 minutes from town to Hapuna Beach, and I went there often, several times a week, before going to work in the afternoon. My mornings at Hapuna were as important for my health, I felt, as brushing my teeth or combing my hair. I just *had* to have a dose of Hapuna. In my busy and hectic life (so it seemed, at the time) as a business owner, Hapuna was necessary for my sanity. Those lovely sun drenched mornings counterbalanced the afternoons of selling art under the influence of double-expressos.

In 1993, Professor Stephen Leatherman, known as "Dr. Beach," named Hapuna the "Best Beach in America." It's definitely a world-class beach. It's pretty much postcard picture perfect. The divinely warm water is clear turquoise; the sands are tawny gold. The beach is wide and long. There's a smoothie bar, picnic benches, and restrooms, and they are not obtrusive. There are outdoor showers surrounded by pretty purple beach morning glories. The Park is well kept and there is plenty of parking. It sort of has a beach boy *California dreamin'* feeling.

Hapuna also has great *mana*, spiritual power. *Ha* in Hawaiian means "breath"; *puna* means "spring."

Hapuna means "breath of life," and is named for the water that bubbles from under the lava rocks at the northern end of the beach. You can see the springs at low tide, and still drink from them with your cupped hands. Greatly revered by the ancients for their powers of rejuvenation, the waters begin high up in Mauna Kea volcano, whose name means "White Mountain," where in the last ice age, glaciers formed. Ice, snow, and rain travel through ancient lava tubes, finally becoming these artesian wells abundant with minerals, proteins and life. Only Hawaiian royalty were permitted to bathe in or drink the sacred water, imbibing its mana, its life force.

Originally inhabited by native Hawaiians, the archaeological remains of old Hawaiian structures still dot the coastline. North of the beach, on the rocky, shoreline trail between the Hapuna Beach Prince Hotel and the Mauna Kea Beach Hotel, you can still see the remains of several walled structures.

Hapuna is certainly special, and many visitors will declare it their favorite beach.

Before the Queen Ka'ahumanu Highway was finished in 1975, allowing easy access to this 61.8-acre beach park, Hapuna was difficult to get to; this seclusion made the beach fairly private. In 1994, construction of the Hapuna Beach Prince Hotel was completed as part of the Mauna Kea Resort, in spite of more than ten years of protests by environmentalists and those who loved the beach. Once a month for years, crowds of people, mostly hippy types, gathered for Hapuna love-ins; there was great live music—it was *the* thing to do. On the other hand, there was a strong need for jobs, and builders with big money swayed those who were promised work. Ultimately, a referendum was held; sadly, the hotel won.

I remember vividly the day the exact distance from the beach to the site of the new hotel was measured; it was low tide—the hotel took every inch, every centimeter, of beach it was legally allowed to take, and that is why today, on one of the most beautiful beaches of the world, once so sacred to the indigenous people, a 5-star hotel sits. Where I once did cartwheels on the sand, a hundred white plastic hotel guest lounging chairs sit.

The new hotel attracts thousands of visitors a year, and has helped to skyrocket the popularity of Hapuna Beach. Today, the beach is visited by an estimated 600,000 people a year, and is one of the most popular destinations of tourists and locals alike.

Wide and long, this gorgeous beach, with its fine soft sand, excellent for building sand castles (and you may see some truly fantastic ones), stretches for several hundred yards. The water is as clear as a beach lover's dream-come-true—absolutely stunning —and its smooth sandy bottom extends out for hundreds of feet.

Boogie boarding is a beloved sport here, because there are *always* rolling waves. A note for the modest —make sure your swimsuit is secure! I repeat, there are *always* rolling waves.

If leisurely strolling a long stretch of beach is your thing, this is the place. If you just want to sunbathe, you can stretch out a towel on the soft sand and take a delightful snooze; make sure to use sunscreen, though; that nap might become longer than you planned. If you're into distance swimming, you can swim a mile down the coast to Wai'alea Bay, Beach 69, and back.

This is a great beach for the kids too, **but watch out—rip tides can take you unawares.** There are lifeguards, but drownings here do happen. Also, once in a while, especially in winter, wind can be a strong factor here; if you've never experienced fierce blowing sand, you are *not* in for a treat.

When water is calm, there is excellent snorkeling toward the south point, along the rocky cliffs and the edges of the bay—you can find lots of fish, coral and probably green sea turtles. This side of the bay is more protected from the open ocean. The reef begins around the point, about a hundred yards out. If you're a beginner snorkeler, head for the rock outcropping just offshore at the middle of the beach. If you're more advanced and the water is calm, head for the right side of the bay, offshore from the hotel, where there are some great coral formations and underwater caves. If you need snorkeling gear, you can rent it for $10 dollars a day from Paradise Grill, located at the top of the hill above the beach, near the parking area.

Be aware that shark sightings are not all *that* rare. Tiger sharks, 12-14 feet long, sometimes enter the bay, for *kicks,* I suppose. The Park has closed at times because of sightings.

Hapuna Point is at the southern end of the beach. The waves far, far out at the left point of Hapuna, because of the very shallow, sharp reef, are very different from the shore break farther in; it only breaks out here when waves are BIG, resulting in breathtaking waves for experienced surfers.

However, beware: it's a long paddle from shore, and out of range of the lifeguards.

Waves can be especially big in winter months, with dangerous rip currents and high surf. Stay out of the water during these times.

Interestingly, a group of U.S. Marines established Camp Henry C. Drewes at Hapuna during World War II. They used this beautiful beach to recover from battle and train for the war from January until May of 1944. A commemorative plaque is located near the parking area.

Want to have a romantic beach wedding? Check with the Hapuna Beach Prince Hotel, which, by the way, offers an *excellent* Sunday brunch. Christmas, Thanksgiving, and Easter Brunch here is always a treat for the gourmand, especially since afterward you can waddle down to the beach and let everything digest while you soak up some sun and nap on the beach.

Camping is not allowed on the beach itself, but for a fairly rustic adventure, completely different from the Hapuna Prince, you might consider renting one of the State Park's six A-frame cabins. They are just on the hill above the beach, about a five-minute walk away. Rustic they are—you'll get two benches to sleep on (no cushions, bring your own), a picnic-table, electricity and outside water. You'll also get mice. There is a shared kitchen facility with a range and refrigerator. Reservations must be made seven days in advance; cost is $30 nightly for Hawaii residents and $50 for non-residents. You can make your reservation here:

https://camping.eHawaii.gov/camping/all, details,1694.html.

The *best* thing about these cabins is that you can leave them, and head down for the beach for a priceless, magical night on one of the beautiful beaches in the world.

I suggest a whole day at Hapuna, if possible. Evenings are special here, and often, around sunset, the crowds are gone, and you can enjoy the feel of walking an incredibly beautiful beach alone while catching the quintessential tropical sunset. A magical end to your wonderful day!

A'ho!

#11
Kiholo

Getting there: Easy to find, no need map! Take Highway 19. At mile-marker 82 off Highway 19 is an overlook with a great view of the sprawling bay. The public access road is on the right between **mile-marker 82 and 83**. The gate is usually open during the week between 8 a.m. and 4 p.m. You'll find a well-maintained, partially paved road for 2.3 miles. You park just steps from the beach where there are toilet facilities or you can make a left for a short distance and park next to an abandoned home, once owned by singer Loretta Lynn. The area just to the south is for camping. If the gate is locked, hike the access road or take the path at mile-marker 81 down to the beach. Both trails take at least 30 minutes to walk. Kiholo Bay is surrounded by private, very expensive, homes, but the beach itself is accessible to the public. Go early in the morning so you can enjoy the best views and get a parking place. Be sure to stay off private property; stick to the coastline, the island, and the ocean. No facilities, no lifeguards. Wear appropriate shoes for the rocky hike, unless you have Hawaiian feet, or want to acquire Hawaiian feet!

Wow! Kiholo beach has it all! Beautiful scenery, tide pools, ancient ponds, rock formations. And a picturesque lava rock island in the heart of the bay. It stretches from Luahinewai Pond at the south end to Wainanali'i Pond at the north end, a full 2 miles. It offers wonderful swimming, snorkeling, spear fishing (Ugh! Not so wonderful), salt gathering, camping, and surfing.

A mixture of fresh and salt water, surrounded by lava rock and dotted with tide pools, the bay was once a fishpond—a wonder of its day—two miles long and six miles wide, with rock walls six feet high, built by King Kamehameha I in 1810, who, it seems, among his other natural talents, was an enterprising engineer. A lava flow from Mauna Loa in 1859 destroyed most of the ancient fishpond.

According to Hawaiian legend, in 1801 when Mount Hualalai erupted, lava was advancing toward Kiholo when King Kamehameha I, to appease the volcano goddess, tossed a pig as sacrifice in its path. Pele, who had come in pursuit of the 'awa and mullet in the fishpond, accepted the offering, and the flow ceased. But in 1859, when Kamehameha was no longer living, Mauna Loa erupted, filling the nearby fishpond with lava. Remains of the pond can still be seen, such as walls and a sluice. When the tide is out, many tide pools dot the bay. When surf is calm, the entire area is terrific for swimming and snorkeling. The tide pools are great for swimming and snorkeling, as they have relatively calm waters compared to the rest of the bay.

Don't forget your binoculars—there are often whales spotted offshore.

The hike from the highway is long and hot; take plenty of water. It's a moderate hike, but you will do a lot of scrambling over rocks and lava. This beautiful bay is an incomparable variation of blues due to the mixture of salt and fresh water. Fresh water flows into the bay through walled streams.

Wainanali'i Pond, a five-acre brackish-water lagoon, is the night resting place of sea turtles. Because of its natural semicircular barrier, the ocean is often calm. The views from the coast are superb.

If you are a hiker, you'll find this area some of the best hiking in the State. Part of the ancient Hawaiian trail system, the Kiholo-Puako trail runs along the contour of the leeward coast. And it is still pristine and undeveloped—running along a two-mile stretch of white pebble and sand beach, lined with palm trees.

Right before the Lookout Point on Highway 19, take the right fork when the road splits. You'll see the old abandoned, round wooden Loretta Lynn house. To the left of the house, you'll find an area to explore —black lava rock that will take you to the Luahinewai pond and the Hualalai flow of 1800.

Luahinewai Pond, one of the Kiholo's main attractions, is a huge, deep freshwater pool located on the southern end of the bay. Known and used by the ancient Hawaiians as a canoe landing and bathing place, it is surrounded by coconut palms, lush vegetation, and a black-sand beach—it's a great place to swim. There are three black sand and pebble beaches near Luahinewai, good for swimming when the water is calm, but take care during high surf. **Especially watch out for rip currents.**

Going north, walking along the well-defined shoreline, just off the shoreline takes you to the lovely Queen's Bath, Keanalele Waterhole, one of my favorite Queen's Baths. The roof of this lava tube filled with water from a spring has collapsed in two places, allowing access to the water, which rises and falls with the tide. You'll have to climb in and out by the ladder.

Hiking north about another 100 yards, you'll come to the front of a very beautiful home, built by the inventor of the heart pacemaker. Here you will find a number of natural rock-edge pools at the ocean's edge.

Continuing a short distance further north, you will come to the Bali House, owned by the creator of the famed Paul Mitchell Hair Products. Lucky guy!

The trail continues on, circling around Kiholo Bay, past more private homes, the ancient Hawaiian fishponds, over two small bridges to the beautiful, shallow, five-acre blue-green lagoon where you will probably see sea turtles basking in the sun on the small rock islands. This is Wainanali'i Pond. It is 10-12 feet deep; it can be seen as a spot of beautiful aqua color from the Lookout Point of Queen Ka'ahumanu Highway.

Past the fishponds, the trail cuts back slightly from the coast and then changes radically. This is the Mauna Kea Lava Flow of 1859; it continues on over the large black lava rock north to where it meets up with the Old King's Highway; it continues north about 10 miles to Puako. This portion of the trail, carved into rock, is rough walking and usually *hot*. Be prepared.

There is another access trail down to the Kiholo Bay section of the trail. Past the Lookout Point, on the ocean side of the road, just past the guardrail at mile-marker 81, is a small dirt trail that never closes. Usually there are a few cars parked here; if not, you can spot it by its large indentation off the road, making parking easy along the highway. This trail takes about 20 minutes to walk, and meets up at the bay at the caretaker's house, a friendly *kane* (man) who might like to talk a little story.

He might tell you that Kiholo, even after the flow of 1859 destroyed most of the pond and changed the coastline dramatically, continued to be occupied by fisher folk. In the 1890's, until 1935, Kiholo was used by the Pu'u Wa'awa'a Ranch as a cattle shipping point. The poor terrified creatures were rowed to steamers offshore. When the cattle began to be shipped from the Kailua pier instead, Kiholo continued on as a small village where cattle, pigs, and fish were raised.

The 1960 tsunami wiped out everything.

After that, the very wealthy discovered it.

For years, Kiholo was a place where those who were in the know could camp. As it became more in the know, and more people camped there, unfortunately the expected happened. People began leaving their trash behind. In October of 2011, Hawaii's Department of Land and Natural resources closed the area, and undertook a major cleanup of this beautiful coastal area. It has now reopened. Camping is now legally allowed, and getting the required permit is relatively easy. You can either go to the State Park office or register online using the Hawaii State Parks Online Reservation System. Now you can be assured of a camping space.

In late December of 2011, seven acres of Kiholo Bay land adjacent to Kiholo State Park were donated to the Nature Conservancy by Angus Mitchell, son of the late Paul Mitchell. This donation ensures that this special Big Island land will remain undeveloped. Like the Park, this land will be cared for by the non-profit group Hui Aloha Kiholo, that is, "those who love Kiholo."

Try to visit Kiholo during a weekday. You possibly will have it all to yourself. Believe it or not!

#12
Honokohau Beach (The Nude Beach), 'Alula Beach and Ai'opio Beach

Getting there: Easy to find. From Kona, take Highway 19 towards the Kona Airport. Just past town, between **mile-markers 97 and 98**, look for the Honokohau Boat Harbor sign at Kealakehe Parkway. After you turn into the harbor road take the first right turn and follow it until you see the Kona Sailing Club. Park in the gravel parking area and, for **Honokohau Beach** look to the right for the park gate. Walk along the trail north and then when you get to the ocean, head to the right.

By the way, remember Gilligan's Island? It was filmed here at the harbor.

For **'Alula Beach**, sometimes called Honokohau Harbor Beach, walk past the park gate, and head for the southern side of the small green park.

For **Ai'opio Beach**, bear to the right and go to the north parking lot. Take the short trail to the beach.

The Park is open year round. Camping is not permitted; dogs are permitted but must be on a leash at all times. (Yeah, right!) For more information about the Park, phone 808-329-6881.

This arid, desolate-looking Park covers a whopping 1160 acres, and includes beachfronts, ancient fishponds and temples, petroglyphs, burial caves, ancient sledding sites, and a segment of the King's highway. In ancient times, this dry volcanic area of lava rock was called *kekah 'a'ole wai* (lands without water).

First: **Ai'opio Beach**, a few yards north of the harbor. This is a small beach with a calm, protected swimming area good for the *keikis* (children) near the archaeological site of Hale o Mono. This temple is still in use today. You may see fruit and flower offerings laid out lovingly—makes a nice photo shoot.

'Alula Beach, named for the endemic plant which looks like a cabbage on a stick, is a small, white, crescent-shaped sand beach, a short walk over lava to the left of the harbor entrance, just north of Ai'opio. On the way to the beach you will see some old stone houses and a heiau. It is a fairly well protected, secluded cove, providing some safe swimming most of the year. Snorkeling is excellent here, and this is a popular entry point for offshore divers as well. The rock walls that plunge 45 feet down into the water create a natural shelter for the fish, and also act as a shield from the tide, creating a safe place for swimmers. Palm and coconut trees line the beach, providing shade and a beautiful view of the Kona coast and harbor activities.

Sweet!

Honokohau Bay means "bay drawing dew," but it has been known for years as "the Nude Beach." It was the favorite hang out of hippies and hippy types during the 70's and 80's, who liked to get the all-over tan while smoking a little weed, trading beach massages, playing Frisbee and eating coconut spoon meat and papaya sprinkled with spirulina or brewer's yeast. Then it became a sort of nude/gay beach, popular with gay men in particular.

"The Nude Beach" is really though, a part of Kaloko-Honokohau National Historical Park, established in 1978, for the preservation, protection and interpretation of traditional native Hawaiian culture.

For some years, nude swimming and sunbathing was ignored, but in recent years, with the rapid development of the Park, the police have set up shop in the bushes, so to speak. It isn't clear whether nudity is actually illegal on this beach, but you can be cited under Federal statues, whatever that means. It's kind of ambiguous; I haven't heard that anyone has actually been arrested.

I was out there one day when the Park rangers first began to enforce their will on the laid-back but recalcitrant hippies. A ranger approached a beautiful, naked, svelte, blond Barbie-doll type who was lying on her tummy sunbathing.

"Nudity is prohibited," he said sternly.

The beautiful Barbie sat up, pointed her breasts innocently at the ranger, and smiled a glowing smile.

"You have to wear a swim suit here," he roared, ignoring her love-is-all-there-is smile, staring instead directly at the bronzed upper ventral region of her torso. "It's the law!"

"Great!" she said, beaming him up with a be-here-now expression, and she reached over for her teeny-weeny itsy bitsy bikini top, tied it on top of her head, stood up, and walked jauntily bare okole (bum) down to the water.

Up until the 19th century, this whole area of Kaloko-Honokohau was a large Hawaiian settlement that provided abundant fishing and access to freshwater and brackish pools. A long salt-and-pepper sand beach, with fragments of seashells, coral and lava rock, Honokohau Beach has a low lava shelf at the water's edge that lines most of the shore. The ocean bottom near the shore is shallow and a bit rocky (you might want to wear reef slippers or tennis shoes in the water), and an offshore reef shelters the beach from strong surf and currents. This is a good place for snorkeling and fairly good for swimming. This is also a good place to watch turtles.

At the southern end of the beach is 'Ai'opio Fishtrap, some anchialine ponds and a heiau. In ancient times, fish swam into an opening in the rock wall at high tide and were trapped inside. This is still a popular shore-fishing site; you'll see fisher folk using nets as well as spears and poles.

For great bird watching, go a short distance north of the beach along the Ala Hele Kekaha Kai path; this is the Aimakapa Fishpond. Among other birds you might see the Hawaiian Coot, Wandering Tattler and Ruddy Turnstone.

If you want, you can walk the Ala Hele Kekaha Kai path all the way to Kaloko Fishpond (*Kaloko* means "pond"). A short distance before Kaloko Pond, there is an old jeep trail, Ala Hele Hu'e Hu'e that leads to Harbor Lefts, a popular secluded surf break for locals. At Kaloko Pond are more restrooms and picnic tables; this is a scenic spot and makes a nice hike. There is a trail around the north side of Kaloko fishpond, Ala Hele Poe Kahiko, which loops around the pond and back, a little longer than a half mile.

Another trail great to hike is the Ala Hele Ike Hawaii trail, scattered with brackish ponds, ancient Hawaiian ruins and petroglyphs. It begins near the restrooms at the entrance gate and goes to the 'Aimakapa Fishpond, the largest wetland on the Big Island. Here you can probably see the Hawaiian duck, the Coot, the Hawaiian Stilt, and the Black-crowned Night Heron. If you continue on the trail, you wind up at the middle gate of the Park, and the visitor center, Hale Ho'okipa. Here there are Park Rangers (if they aren't out in the bush, watching for "activities"), a gift shop, bathrooms, and the only drinking water in the Park. It is a half-mile from Honokohau Beach to the Park Center, which is open from 8:30 to 4 p.m. daily.

My favorite thing about this beach is the beautiful Queen's Bath here. Yes, another Queen's bath. Seems wherever a brackish or freshwater pool was found, it instantly became the Queen's. This one is a little difficult to find but well worth the effort. This one is my favorite of all the Queen's Baths.

Walk to the northern end of the beach. Look carefully and you'll see a trail across the lava. Walk approximately 600 feet north from the northern end of the beach toward the mountains. You'll see some mysterious rock cairns made from the lava. No one knows who built them or what they were for, but it has been guessed that they were for sentinels for the queen. The Queen's Bath is located right behind the rock mounds, encircled by Christmas Berry trees.

This is a spring-fed lava pool. The pool is linked to the ocean and rises and falls according to the tides.

If you are lucky, you will have it all to yourself. Magical!

However, it is now, unlike in the old days, *kapu*, forbidden, to swim in the bath.

Honokohau is hot and dry. Like in the old days, it is still *kekah 'a'ole wai*. You probably will need a hat, as well as lots of water and sunscreen. You might prefer to visit in the early morning or later in the afternoon, when it's usually overcast. Keep in mind that the trails are mostly over bare lava fields, so good shoes are advised.

As a matter of historical interest, it is speculated that the bones of Kamehameha were buried in secret near Kaloko.

No wonder this place has such mana.

#13
Halape

I wish I had a tiny island floating in the sea
Palm trees don't get in the way, it's a tropical ease
And everywhere that I keep my silence, no sound returns to me
Just endless waves at the end of our days, the sighing of the seas
But yesterday's gone, I don't know where I come from, hmmm
Wonder where I'm going

Remember that poignant song by Leo Kottke? He must have been dreaming of Halape.

Remote? You say you want a remote beach? Breathtaking? Did you say you want to find a *really* breathtaking beach?

Halape is as about remote and breathtaking as you can get on the Big Island.

Getting there: Halape is on the southern sea coast of Hawaii Volcanoes National Park. Getting there is not easy, to say the least. In fact, this is the most remote beach in my list of best beaches. But if you can make it, this will be an experience you will *never* forget, the memory of a lifetime. Plan on at least two days.

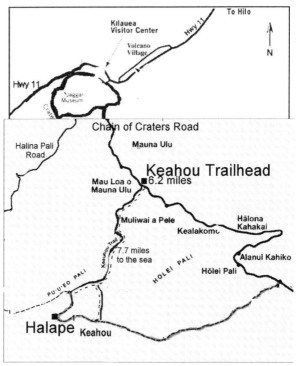

This trip is recommended **for very experienced backpackers only.** Plan on camping because as grueling as it is to descend down the 7.7 miles and 2200 feet to the sea, it is more challenging to get back up, duh! The knees! This is one of the few places camping is legal along the Park's Puna Coast Trail.

You **must** register the day before your hike with the Backcountry Office of Hawaii Volcanoes National Park; reservations are *not* accepted. You may camp a maximum of three nights. You may register and get information and maps by calling 808-985-6178. **Study the maps**, **talk to the rangers** before doing this one!

Halape is accessed through a grueling hot hike from Mau Loa o Mauna Ulu, also called the Keauhou Trail, via the Chain of Craters Road in Hawaii Volcanoes National Park. Park in the vehicle turnout for the Mau Loa o Mauna Ulu trailhead (odometer 6.2) on the right (elev. 2,680 ft). You can get a free map at the Park Visitor Center.

There are two other ways to access it but they are even more grueling: the Hilina Pali Trail, accessed via Hilina Pali Road, and Puʻu Loa via the Puna Coast Trail, accessed via Chain of Craters Road. I won't give details here, but you can ask the rangers if you really want to rough it.

Beginning at the Mau Loa o Mauna Ulu trailhead, (there actually isn't much of a trail), follow the *ahu*, the lava rock cairns, which lead across the desolate pahoehoe flows from the 1969-74 eruption of Mauna Ulu. *Pahoehoe* is the smooth, ropey lava. At the edge of the flow is a sparse woodland of ʻohia, pukiawe, and other scrubby plants on old flows of mixed pahoehoe and *aʻa*, that's the razor sharp lava. You will wind around razorback passages in the Polo Keawe Pali (*Pali* means "cliff"). The trail descends down markedly through the Ainahou Ranch land. Soon the shoreline comes into view.

Stay on the trail! The trail is steep and very rocky in places, and the ahu may be hard to discern on misty days or rainy days, and most certainly at night. Night hiking is *not* recommended.

There are no trees or shelter from the usually fierce sun, so be prepared. Temperatures may soar into the nineties! **High humidity, strong winds and**

high temperatures can lead to dehydration, heat exhaustion and stroke. On the other hand, you might experience cold wind and rain; hypothermia may be a problem.

Just to let you know.

You will need three to four quarts of water per person per day. You will need sunglasses, sunscreen, a hat and food. Leave early in the day and rest during the hottest part of the day. Park rangers also list the following as essential equipment: first aid kit, trail map, emergency food supply, flash light, toilet paper, signaling device such as a mirror, good hiking shoes, tent, sleeping bag and rain gear and water purification tablets. Do not drink untreated water!

So you can see this is not normally a day trip!

Real dangers include the possibility of earthquakes, rock falls, and tsunamis. For example, in 1975, a 7.2 earthquake rocked Kalapana, causing part of the Ka'u-Puna coast to subside nearly 20 feet. Then, the ensuing 47-foot high tsunami swept over Halape and killed two campers and injured more. Earthquakes are common—native Hawaiian villages which were once situated here were abandoned following the great series of devastating tsunamis about 150 years ago. If you feel a quake, there is a real danger of tidal waves—**head upslope immediately**!

There was, until the 1975 tsunami, a 2.5-acre islet just off the coast of Halape, Keaoi. The tsunami caused Keaoi islet to sink about 10 feet. Once a haven for birds, it is now almost gone, but still juts its head above water at low tide. I think it is about a mile and a half out; I don't know anyone who has snorkeled to it.

Other hazards are the possibility of volcanic eruptions, volcanic gas emissions, and falling into earth cracks, thin crusts, or lava tubes, which are numerous. Besides this, because of the dryness of the area, there is a danger of fire. **Fires of any kind, including smoking, are strictly prohibited**. You may also encounter centipedes, scorpions, black widow spiders, sharks and sea urchins. And last but not least, there is a slight possibility of running upon unexploded WWII unexploded ordinance.

Just to let you know.

Halape has a three-walled primitive shelter, as does your other choice, Keahou. They are about 1.6 miles apart. See the map and talk to the Park rangers about your options. Water caught off the roof is stored in an adjacent catchment tank—check with Park Rangers when you obtain your permit for current water levels—water is NOT always available. The water obtained from catchment tanks *must* be treated before drinking.

Please use the composting toilet. Do not put trash in the toilet. Cart out all your trash, of course.

So, after all these preliminaries of getting there, what can you expect?

A slice of heaven? The garden of Eden? A paradise oasis?

You might call Halape any of these. Few ever will have the sacred privilege of laying their eyes on this beautiful white sand beach complete with coconut trees, sheltered tide pools and pounding surf, shaded by coconut and milo trees.

Lounge in the sun, nap in the shade, hike, snorkel, sleep under the stars, surf...some surfers in the know swear this is their favorite surfing site. Of course, you have to carry your board down and up.

A little further down the coast you can explore Halape Iki, which is a beautiful cove for snorkeling and swimming. There is a very beautiful earth crack pool of deep blue water located in the rift behind the sandy cove. To get there, hike past Halape toward the southwest and follow the white chunks of coral across the black lava for about a mile. About 60 feet long, 12 feet wide, and 10 feet deep, it is mostly fresh water, punctuated by huge boulders that have fallen into the lovely transparent water. The brackish pool is located behind the shelter at Halape at the bottom of a crack along a fault line at the base of Mauna Kapukapu. You can swim in the pool and hang out in the shade of the grove of kou trees, with their orange flowers.

Before the tsunami of 1975, a large grove of coconut trees ringed the cove. Eventually, after the cove dropped into the water and the palms were inundated by the salt water, they toppled and someone, no one knows who, carved them into tikis. You'll remember them forever; they stand like so many sentinels guarding this lovely spot. Be sure and take a picture.

There is also a papamu, a stone surface used for the traditional Hawaiian game called konane.

Halape! For the adventurous!

I wish I had a tiny island floating in the sea
Palm trees don't get in the way, it's a tropical ease

And everywhere that I keep my silence, no sound returns to me
Just endless waves at the end of our days, the sighing of the seas

#14
Waipi'o
(Curved Water)

Getting there: It's about two hours from Kona, and about 1.5 hours from the Kohala resorts or Hilo.

From Hilo, take Highway 19 north. Make a right turn onto State Highway 240 (Waipi'o Road). This road leads to the Waipi'o Valley Lookout.

From Kona, you can either take the coastal road, Highway 19 to Waimea, or the upper road, the Hawaii Belt, Highway 190. To take the upper road, head north into Kona on Highway 11. At the Palani Road intersection, turn right and head up the mountain on Highway 190. In Waimea, go straight through all the signaled intersections and travel on out of town on the same road, now Highway 19, 15 miles to Honokaa. Follow the sign after the 44-mile-marker indicating a left turn into Honokaa. Go down the mountain one mile to Highway 240 and take a left at the 4-way stop following the signs to Waipi'o Valley Lookout.

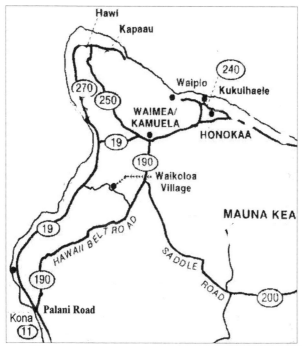

If you want to get some local grinds before going down, try the locally famous Tex Drive-in. They serve the locally famous, much beloved "plate-lunch," and are locally famous for their malasada, which is a sort of heart attack-inducing deep-fried donut. Tex Drive-in is located in Honokaa.

Along with *kau kau* (pronounced cow-cow, the all-purpose, ubiquitous Hawaiian pidgin word for "food"), you might want to take insect repellant. Waipi'o mosquitoes are BIG!

Route 240 dead ends at the parking lot of the Waipi'o Lookout. The spectacular scenic outlook is one of the most photographed vistas in Hawaii. Be sure you have your camera. If you look carefully, you can see the old mule trail off in the distance. If you have a keen eye, you might see waterspouts forming out at sea. There is a park ranger stationed at the left of the road that leads down to the valley; you can get information there.

Be aware there are NO services in Waipi'o. There is no food to buy, no drinking water, no lifeguards!

Jurassic Park?

Think Shangri-La! You may feel you have entered into that mystical, mythical land when you visit Waipi'o, the "Valley of the Kings," so called because it was once one of the most important residences of the royalty of Hawaii. This land was also believed to be the home of many ancient gods who chose it for its grandeur and largesse.

You too will fall under the spell of this seemingly enchanted mile-wide valley, walled in by enormously high cliffs (2000 feet high!), with a luscious and pure river twisting from the Kohala Mountains down to the sea. Taro patches, coconut, avocado, mango, guava and passion fruit trees dot the landscape. Beautiful waterfalls cascade down from the cliffs, and the verdant rainforest is host to a fabulous diversity of natural flora and fauna. Flowers of impatience, six inches tall on the mainland, grow six feet tall here! Elephant ears are the size of Volkswagens! Wild horses run up and down the beach, and at times, dolphins sport just offshore the gleaming black sand beach. The beach is one of the most secluded, accessible beaches of the Big Island.

Before Captain Cook arrived in 1778, some say that as many as 50,000 people lived in this Garden of Eden. Indeed, it was one of the most important cultural centers of the Islands. Today only about fifty lucky people live here.

One of those lucky people is my friend. He hand-carried lumber down the unbelievably steep (25% incline) road, which descends 1000 feet in only a mile, bit by bit, in order to build the tiny but very comfortable hut he now lives in. One side of his hut is built into the rock side of the valley, down which a continuous stream of water flows. This is his running water. There is no electricity or phone surface down in the valley. His toilet is a five-gallon bucket, which he composts around the fruit trees he has been planting for the last 30 years. Talk about self-sustainable! He needs few clothes, basically a bathing suit and a pareo. Actually, he only needs those when he goes "out." He parks his old VW van at the top of the Waipi'o lookout for his trips into town. Being a vegetarian, he has few other needs. He lives on just a few dollars a year. Forever sun-bronzed, sleek and fit, he spends his carefree days swimming, surfing, gardening, and talking story with the taro farmers who live in the valley as his neighbors, and sometimes with visitors to the valley.

Lucky fellow!

Located along the Hamakua Coast on the northeastern coast of the Big Island, Waipi'o Valley is the largest and southernmost of the seven valleys on the windward side of the Kohala Mountains. Besides being one of the most important sites of ancient temples, its steep cliffs contain the burial caves of royalty.

Access to Waipi'o Beach is not for the faint hearted, as the one-lane, hair-pinned curve road down to the valley hugs the cliff, and even though it is paved (somewhat), you must have a four-wheel drive to navigate it, or, you can choose to walk. Also, you should know that most of the car rental companies prohibit driving down this road.

I always walk it. No way would I get into a car to go down that road! And just so you know I am not exaggerating, the fact is, people have lost their lives on the road, due to failing breaks. At any rate, whatever you decide, be aware that once you start down, you have no choice—it is impossible to turn around on the narrow road. **Check your brakes carefully! Before starting down.** You can see for yourself the rusting graveyard of trucks at the bottom of the ravine. The rule of the road here is that the car coming up has the right of the way, and you should make room by pulling to the side. The road is barely big enough for one full-sized SUV; therefore look sharp! If you decide to walk down, you can park your car at the Waipi'o lookout.

You can also choose to visit Waipi'o by horseback. In this case, you meet your horse at The Last Chance Store in Kukuihaele. Tours are offered Monday-Saturday twice daily, and must be reserved at least one day in advance. The number is 808-775-7291.

Waipi'o Naalapa Stables, 808-775-0419, also offers horseback adventures in the valley. Be sure and take your ride a banana.

ATV tours are also offered, but I refuse to promote the horribly noisy creatures. They just don't belong in paradise.

There is also a shuttle tour, called appropriately Waipi'o Valley Shuttle. Call 808-775-7121. Reservations are recommended.

Then there is the Waipi'o Valley Wagon Tour. If the idea of a mule-drawn covered wagon is your thing, call 808-775-9518. Reservations required. Also take a banana.

I would suggest though, if you really want to spend some time there, walk down and walk out. Be aware though, it is a steep climb up; your calves and thighs will definitely get a work out. You will be rewarded, however, with magnificent vistas and great photographic opportunities, plus, you'll expend a few thousand extra calories, so you can afford that oily heart attack-inducing malasada from Tex Drive-in.

Whether you walk down or drive down (good luck!), from the bottom of the paved road, there is a fork. Hike ten minutes to the east (right) to get to the black sand beach that runs almost the entire length of the shoreline of the valley. Access to the beach is easier to make on the way upward to the left, rather than to make a sharp right hand turn as you descend. You'll see what I mean when you get there.

More often than not, violent surf pounds the coast here, especially in winter. Be forewarned, I repeat, *be forewarned*—even though the beach is idyllically beautiful, with its spectacular cliffs and tumbling cascades, **there are *intense* rip currents here** that flow out to sea, and the surf is *strong*. *Gnarly* is the word. Swimmers should use extreme caution; avoid swimming unless the surf is very calm. There are no lifeguards here; you are on your own. Swimming during winter months is especially ill advised as very strong waves break along this shoreline. There are also rock hazards. Take all postings and warnings to heart.

If you don't want to chance it, there is a small stream flowing into the ocean where you and the keikis (if you have some) can play, but even here, watch out for rising waters. Rains above can swell this stream into a raging river. Sometimes cars transverse this river; sometimes they try and don't make it. I knew of someone who tried to get across in a brand new Suzuki Samurai—it got stuck, he never could get it out, and had to continue making car payments until it was paid for. It is still there rusting in the stream.

As for surfing, the locals surf early, before 8:30 a.m. when the trades perk up. But this is definitely a place for experts. Surfers surf all year long here. Offshore winds are from the southwest and the best swells are from the northeast. Even when there are waves, it's never crowded.

During the winter, this is a great place to watch the humpback whales, as they pass by offshore.

Before you reach the beach, you will see a forest and very possibly wild horses. Some are quite responsive to humans—maybe you can remember to take them an apple or a carrot? Hiking on eastward, two sparkling waterfalls come into view, Kaluahine Falls, and then Waiulili falls. There's a trail to Kaluahine Falls, a rough trail along the lava rocks that runs from the intersection of the cliffs and the ocean to the falls. It's about an hour one way.

If instead of going east at the fork in the road, you hike west (left), you can hike to a fabulous view of Hiilawe Falls, the highest in Hawaii at 1400 feet. Sometimes this "road" is washed out. If it isn't, you can hike deep into the Valley till you reach its remote northwest wall. It's about two and half hours one-way. It's pretty much a bushwhacking adventure, with streams to cross and a forest to traverse. There is only a faint path that zigzags, crossing two barbed-wire fences. Don't drink the water or walk into it with open sores or cuts; leptospirosis is a real danger. I know someone who died of it.

It's about a 90-minute hike to the falls, and on the way you will see The Teahouse, an abandoned building that was to be a restaurant, now quickly being reclaimed by the jungle. It was built in the sixties, but apparently the wife of the entrepreneur took one look at it and refused to go along with his plans. It is now owned by the Bishop Museum.

Camping is technically not allowed in the Valley. However, if you want the ultimate camping experience, you can get a free backcountry camping permit from the Division of Forestry and Wildlife to camp in remote Waimanu Valley, one valley over from Waipi'o; you'll need at least three days for this amazing adventure. The switchback Muliwai Trail begins at the western end of Waipi'o beach, opposite the stream from the Waipi'o lookout. The panoramas are incredible, surpassing even the view of Waipi'o. During heavy rains, the trail is very treacherous.

The trail begins at the valley floor by taking the road to the right, following the beach to Wailoa Stream, fording the stream, and then following the horse trail on the dunes to the west side of the Valley. It climbs 1200 feet, and then leads across a plateau, crossing 12 gulches that are as deep as 500 feet, and then it descends another 1200 feet into Waimanu Valley. **It is for experienced and fit hikers.** Watch out for wild pigs, and do not try to cross swollen streams! The hike itself is approximately 10 hours in and 10 hours out. Get information from the Forestry and Wildlife Division at 808-974-4221.

Waipi'o is indeed magical. Legends say that the Valley is haunted by Night Marchers, *huaka'i po*, the ghosts of long-dead warrior armies. They march on certain nights of the moon, notably *Po Kane*, a night of no moon, and *Po Akua*, the fourteenth night of the new moon. Their march is accompanied often by heavy winds, fog, mist, rain and lightening, and most often they march to the beat of haunting drums and by the light of torches. There may also be a putrid smell in the air, and the haunting sound of a conch shell being blown, and sometimes an eerie clanging can be heard. Some say they float a few inches from the ground, but others claim they leave footsteps.

If you see the phantom army of Night Watchers, you must lie down on the ground on your tummy and avert your eyes. Otherwise, a grim fate awaits you.

Legends, and local inhabitants, also tell of mysterious fireballs, sometimes bluish-green orbs and sometimes gleaming white orbs, which are shot from one side of the Valley to the other. These are *akualele*. Some say they are the spirits of unworthy souls, but most often they are said to be either the weapons of battling kahunas, Hawaiian sorcerers, or the omen of coming death to whoever is unfortunate to have one fall nearby. Many, many people have claimed to see them. To protect yourself, if you should happen to see one, you should start cursing it. Fireballs don't like cursing, for some reason.

As I mentioned before, high up on the steep sides of the cliffs are ancient burial caves of royalty. It is believed that the mana of their bones, the spiritual power, is absorbed back into the earth, thus protecting those who live in the valley from harm. In fact, even though Waipi'o was hit by tsunamis in 1946 and 1979, no one died.

At one time, from the late 1800's, many Chinese immigrants lived in the Valley. There were churches, schools, restaurants and even a hotel, post office and jail. But the 1946 tsunami, the worst in Hawaii's history, devastated the Valley, with the waves sweeping to the far side of the Valley walls; after that, many people left.

Then, in 1979, a tsunami deluged the valley from side to side in 40 feet of water! Most of the rest of the people left, as it was realized that the mouth of Waipi'o Valley acts as a funnel for tsunamis, causing them to back up into the valley.

Waipi'o is steeped in Hawaiian history. It was the capital of many of the early Hawaiian kings. It was a place celebrated for its mysterious *nioi* grove, which apparently surrounded or grew nearby the ancient grass palace of the kings. In the 18th century, the chief Kahekili raided Waipi'o, and burned down the sacred trees.

According to legend, three gods entered with a flash of lightening into a grove of harmless trees on the slop of Monanalua on the island of Molokai. The trees were thus imbued with a strange power, and contact with their wood resulted in death. A way was finally found to carve the poisonous wood. Thus, images from the wood must have been imbibed with great spiritual power. How the trees were brought to Waipi'o and by whom, is not known. The burning down of the sacred trees must have been a real psychological victory for Kahekili.

The great king Kamehameha, as a baby, was hidden here in the Valley when his mother fled with him to the safety of her relatives. He spent his childhood here, and it was here that he received his war god Kukailimoku.

Indeed, many Hawaiians view the Valley as the cradle of Hawaiian civilization. In 1994, two woven caskets containing the remains of ancient kings were stolen from the Bishop Museum, and it is strongly suspected that they were secretly buried somewhere in the Valley.

It's almost unbelievable that no Donald Trump or some such creature has conceived the idea to "develop" the Valley. For now, going to Waipi'o is still a dream come true, the chance to experience the magic of the Island as it has been for centuries.

There is no lodging in Waipi'o Valley, but there are several bed and breakfasts just above the Valley. If you have the time, I suggest that you stay at one and explore Waipi'o during the course of a few days. Walking down, of course.

And if you see a sun-bronzed guy with long blond hair wearing a pareo and a satisfied smile, give him my "aloha."

#15
Kahalu'u

Getting there: No need map! Kahalu'u Beach Park is south of the heart of Kailua-Kona town on Ali'i Drive, near the **five mile-marker**, just south of Magic Sands Beach and near the Outrigger Keauhou Beach Resort. This beach has most all the amenities —a concession stand with snorkeling gear rental, lifeguards, bathrooms, showers. It is baby stroller accessible too! You can even stroll over and have an economical lunch at the nearby Outrigger Resort; it serves sandwiches and the much beloved Hawaiian "plate lunch," which is a plate of food heaped to the very top with all the most beloved Hawaiian foods including at least two scoops of white rice.

Also, if you have the keen desire, you can sign up for surfing lessons!

At first sight you might find it strange that Kahalu'u Beach Park is so high up on my list of the best beaches on the island. Located right on the side of Ali'i Drive in a busy part of Kailua town, small and usually crowded, rocky with coarse sand, you might wonder why I love this beach so much. Traffic is zooming by, the parking lot is packed, and kids and their parents are screaming their heads off.

Why do I like this beach?

Kahalu'u is fun, that's why.

Also, if you are an archeology buff, like I am, there are lots of ancient ruins on this beach and immediately surrounding it. You can swim and snorkel, sunbathe and read, have fun watching the turtles and tourists (I have had hours of amusement watching the tourists here, many who are first-time snorkelers, and overhearing their exclamations of sheer joy), and then, wander around and explore the fantastic ruins of the area.

How many Sunday mornings I have spent at this beach! I always go early on Sundays, before the lifeguards come on. You wouldn't believe how beautiful and solitary it is at those hours. (I'm talking 6-7 a.m.) I always stretch out for a few minutes and soak up the first warm rays of the sun coming over the mountain and through the palm trees, because, at that hour, coming down from up *mauka* (up the mountain), my bones need warming up. Then I get my snorkel, wade through the small rocks at the beginning of the beach, and lower myself down into the shallow water to head out toward the Menehune Rocks.

The moment my head is underwater, reality is transformed. I have entered the magical world of Nemo.

Swimming all around me, as if we are all together in a huge, colorful aquarium, are hundreds of finned creatures with such incredible names as raccoon butterfly fish**,** yellow tang, orange band surgeonfish, Picasso triggerfish, orange spine unicorn butterfly fish, Hawaiian ruby cardinal fish, exclamation point dragonet, pink tail triggerfish, disappearing wrasse, sunrise hogfish, big scale squirrelfish, clear fin needle fish, Michael's Ghost goby, painted frog fish, side spot goatfish, peacock grouper, sunset basslet, Schindler's infant fish, barred knife jaw, flowery flounder, moon fish, Moorish idol, cushion star pearl fish, giant porcupine fish, lantern toby, stripe belly puffer, Cookie's sandburrower, red spotted sand perch, galactic scorpion fish, Hawaiian green lion fish, convict tang, the thick-lipped trevally, and of course, the famed State fish, the Humuhumunukunukuapua'a.

There are teeny tiny fish the size of a dime and there are fish easily a yard long. There are puffer fish eight inches wide! There are unimaginable dazzling rainbow colors and unbelievable patterns that stretch one's third eye; our creator really showed his/her skill here. The creatures glide by me, seemingly going about their business like so many people going to work or shopping on Park Avenue, only their world is infinitely more sensual. Or sometimes a frantic critter will suddenly burst by, hotly pursued by a fish that looks all the world like a gangster. For the most part they don't seem to notice that I exist, but once in a while some interesting shape swims by and gives me a haughty sidelong glance.

Kahalu'u Beach is not a marine preserve and has no fishing limitations, yet this tiny sheltered cove in the heart of Kailua town surpasses the quantity of fish you'd see at a dedicated marine sanctuary. This is why Kahalu'u is ranked #8 of 193 things to do on the Big Island by Lonely Planet. Many tourists actually go away believing that the State or the County, someone, planted all these delightful creatures here for the tourists own enjoyment.

Kahalu'u's cove is mostly less than neck deep, which means that the sunlight penetrates all the way to the bottom, permitting the growth of lots of healthy coral. This coral is the food garden of these fish. Besides this, due to the cove being almost completely surrounded by a submerged rock wall, large waves are kept out, allowing in the flow of gentle ocean currents, which carry in an abundance of life-bringing nutrients. According to Hawaiian legend, the ancient breakwater was built on the reef by the *Menehune*, a mythical race of little people, to protect the bay. The breakwater is a combination of natural features and man-made wall. It predates the 15th century temple complexes in the area. It was reported already in disarray at the time of European contact in the 18th century. If you should snorkel all the way out to the breakwater, you will be astounded at the huge boulders that were set into place by ...the *little* people?

If you swim beyond the breakwater, past the boulders, the ocean drops off dramatically, and changes from light green turquoise to the deepest shades of blue.

Kahalu'u means "Bay of the Fishes," though it is called often "Snorkeler's Beach," and also sometimes "Kids' Beach." The water is almost always calm, and is fed by a fresh water spring, estimated at 10 million gallons each day.

Bring your underwater camera, or get one of those inexpensive disposable underwater cameras, for this beach for sure! The fish are incredibly tame, and will swim right up to you. In years past, before rules prohibited the feeding of the fish, people often came here and fed them frozen green peas. The fishies have never forgotten that hand that once fed them!

Of course, besides the fish, there are assorted eels and, to your delight, the turtles will almost brush you with their flippers as they glide by or float in the small surf. This is a fantastic place for beginner snorkelers as well as seasoned experts. The water is calm and safe.

That's because King Kamehameha wanted a safe place for his own family to enjoy, and so he had the seawall built to protect the small cove. Surrounded by shady palm trees, the salt-and-pepper sand is course and gritty; when the tide goes out, rock flats form shallow tide pools.

Don't try to walk on the rocks to get to the water. They are covered with slippery seaweed, which, besides making walking on them treacherous, makes you look clumsily ridiculous. Some people wear reef shoes or tennis shoes into the water; there are lots of rocks and spiny urchins here. Not only that, but the *honu*, the sea turtles, like to bask on the rocks; careful you don't mistake one for a stone. When they dry in the sun, their shells look amazingly just like the rocks. Sometimes you might see groups of people standing together and looking at something on the rocks. Yep! They are looking at a sleeping turtle.

You can get into the water through a couple of sandy patches; one is almost right in front of the lifeguard's stand and the other is on the north side of the pavilion. Carry your fins and put them on in the water for an easier time of it. Then just float out.

The water closest to the shore is usually stirred up if lots of people are on the beach. Head out further for clearer water.

Don't rush the fish or chase them to get a picture. No matter how slow a fish seems to be going, you can't possibly outrace them anyhow. **Don't stand on the reef; it is easily destroyed.** It's illegal as well as the height of bad beach manners to stand on the reef. You'll definitely get stink eye. Try not to scream and shout in your excitement. Be on the lookout for other snorkelers; it's easy to jab someone with an elbow or kick someone in the face. Also, be wary of spear fishers; sadly, spear fishing is still permitted here, unbelievably. I have been made very uncomfortable by these killers swimming close beside me with those long spear guns and sinister grins on their faces.

If you swim north of the pavilion, watch out for surfers. This is an ancient surf spot that is still popular with the locals. **The Ku'emanu Heiau**, with its anu'u platform, used by royalty to view surfing, is here on the north end. Back in the days, only the *ali'i* (royalty) were allowed to surf, you see. Be sure to stroll over and see it. It's perhaps the only temple in the world dedicated solely to surfing. Ku'emanu was also a *luakini* heiau, a temple of human sacrifice, and on the north side of it is a *laupa'u*, a bone pit where human remains were thrown. It is still much revered; please do not touch it or disturb it in any way. This spot makes a great photograph.

On a lighter note, the surfing school is right across the street.

If you are eager to learn to surf, check out the Kona Surf Company ahead of time at 808-217-5329. *Hue o he'e nalu!* Surf's up!

Nearby is a brackish pond called Waiku'i, which means "pounding water," where the ali'i rinsed off the salt water.

The quaint little blue church, known commonly as, you guessed it, "the little blue church," sits on the site of a former kahuna's house. Its formal name is "Saint Peter's by the Sea," and it was built in 1880 on La'aloa Bay (Magic Sands Beach, just up the road) and moved here in 1912. It has been moved from its foundation twice by tsunamis, but it's a survivor. It can be rented for weddings, in case you are interested. I can't imagine a wedding in a more delightful spot, can you?

Right across the streets you will see some ruins covered by vines. This is Helani Church, built in 1861 by the Rev. John Paris. . Beneath it are the ruins of 'Ohi'a-Mukumuku Heiau, said by the ancients to have been built by the gods. It was dedicated to the fearsome Kuka'ilimoku, the war god, by Lonoikamakakahiki of Hawaii Island, so that he might vanquish his Maui enemy.

The legend is impressive and details the great wars in the 16th century between Hawaii and Maui. At one point, when Kamalalawallu, the chief of Maui attacked Hawaii, the number of canoes was so vast that the first canoes were landing on Hawaii before the last of their canoes were leaving Maui.

This fierce chief of Maui had two huge, fierce dogs, a white one named Kapapaki and a black one named Kauakahioka'oka, who accompanied him into battle.

Finally, though, Lonoikamakakahiki gained the ascendancy. Kamalalawallu was sacrificed alive at the nearby Ke'eku Heiau by first being staked to the ground for days, tortured, and then butchered on a nearby rock, after which he was fed to the sharks. It was said his dogs were also staked to the ground, one on each side of him, and subjected to the same treatment. There are some ghost stories that purport that the dogs can still sometimes be seen roaming about here, howling for their master.

The **Ke'eku Heiau** is over at the Outrigger Hotel on the south side of the beach. Its walls were 6-11 feet thick. On its raised stone platform are two stone features representing the two war dogs. There are also petroglyphs, *ki'i pohaku*, in the rocks in the intertidal area in front of the heiau that are said to represent the sacrificed king. Directions to it are below.

Paokamenehune Seawall, a partly natural, partly man-made sea wall, encloses the south end of Kahalu'u Bay. Paokamenehune predates the 15th century temple complexes in the area and is held in legend to have been built by the menehune. It actually was built by the chiefs to encircle a large fishpond. The breakwater was already crumbling at the time of European contact in the 18th century. I have often sat on top of it for my morning meditation, the waves lapping just below my feet.

Between the two park pavilions is an ancient canoe landing. Mokuahi'ole, an important heiau and residence of royalty, once was located where the large pavilion is today. Ka'ahumanu, the favorite queen of Kamehameha, and perhaps Hawaii's first feminist, was raised here.

Kahalu'u is one of my favorite places to go during a big storm, not to swim, but just to watch. I've seen magnificent waves roll over the wall and over Ali'i Drive. I repeat, during storms, this is a great place to watch, but don't try getting into the water

When surf is up, Kahalu'u can harbor strong rip currents that pull northward into the rocks. Quite a few drownings have taken place here, because people get so absorbed in snorkeling and venture out too far in the current. Just to let you know, too, it is not uncommon for people to die of heart attacks and drown here. That's because they're not in good physical shape, they're excited, they are on vacation and thus, often, eating and drinking way over the top. I've seen drownings with my own eyes, sadly. Be wary of getting caught in this current. The good news is the lifeguards here are very vigilant and well trained. I've watched many rescues.

There are clean restrooms, and an old-fashioned shave ice truck opens at 9 a.m., about the time people start arriving, including the lifeguards. There are cold outdoor, I mean c-o-l-d, showers, picnic tables and two pavilions. The entire pavilions can be reserved free of charge through the county for birthday parties and things like that. If parking in the lot is filled, you can park on the street opposite the beach.

The south end of the bay became Kahalu'u' Beach County Park in 1953. The area around the bay was added to the National Register of Historic Places in 1974.

I remember when it was common and not illegal for people to camp at Kahalu'u. Back in the seventies, hippies lived here in colorful tents, lounging about in hammocks, playing with their naked babies in the sand, smoking pot and strumming guitars. Today, besides the tourists, the locals still hang out here, and local fisher folk still fish off the lava rocks over by the hotel. If you come here early in the morning, or at sunset, when the light is beautiful and rich, you might get some wonderful photos of net fishers silhouetted against the sky.

Kahalu'u is rich in Hawaiian history and one of Hawaii's most culturally significant sites. The ahupua'a of Kahalu'u, named for a high-ranking chiefess, was an important royal residence in the 18th and 19th centuries. This area was densely populated even back in the old days; besides all the advantages of the life-giving ocean and its abundant fishing grounds, the area's upslope topography was the birther of evening rains, providing precious fresh water. The Paokamenehune, the wall of the ancients, was a technological engineering feat of its day. Besides, there were almost ten heiau situated here.

This is a wonderful, history-filled place to explore on foot.

The old Keauhou Beach hotel, built in 1970, now called the Outrigger Beach Resort, is just next door, and all around it are ancient historical sites. The hotel doesn't mind a bit if you walk through barefooted and in your bathing suit; they are used to it. You'll see a gate on the south side of the beach. You can walk right in and meander around the sidewalks, reflecting on the sacred stone temples that have been restored.

This old hotel is my favorite hotel on the island. It is just so unpretentious.

The small point of land *makai* (toward the sea) of the swimming pool is the Kapuanoni Heiau, dedicated to fishing. Po'o Hawaii Pond, just a few yards to the east, is a rare freshwater spring that was strictly reserved for the use of the ali'i as a fish and bathing pond. You can see the two *pohaku ku'ula*, the fishing stones, where, in the past, offerings were left here for good luck. The stones were brought here from Maui in double-hulled canoes long ago. They have names, Kanaio and Ulupalakua. In the larger of the two stones you can see the images of a turtle, shark, and fishhook. See the round hole near the top? That means it was a luakine stone, a stone for human sacrifice—a rope was passed through the hole and around the victim's neck and the victim was strangulated.

Just north of the heiau is the sacred bathing pool, Poho'okapo. Walk right through the lobby of the hotel until you see the paved path at the end of the driveway. You will pass Punawai Spring at the end of the tennis courts, a rare and precious freshwater spring, said to be a fertility spring where young girls bathed to promote fertility. Ironically, even today wedding ceremonies take place here in this beautiful glade.

Also here is the Mo'o twins' home site. *Mo'o* means "lizard." The Mo'o Twins were prophetesses of the lizard goddess. They were famous for their singing and healing arts. Today turtles often bask in their tide pool.

Keep walking until the path ends at the broken concrete bridge; this is Hapaiali'i Heiau, an astrological temple built between 1411 and 1465. It seems to have been a solar calendar—on winter solstice, from a viewing point directly behind the temple's center stone, the sun sets directly off the southwest corner of the heiau; at the vernal equinox, the sun sets directly along the centerline of the temple, and at summer solstice, it sets off the northwest corner. Some historians say it was also a temple for "elevating chiefs," involving changes in rank. It was said to have taken thousands of commoners over ten years to build. It is completely built by dry-stack masonry, without mortar. The heiau was reconstructed in 2007 by Kamehameha schools.

Hapai means "pregnant," and *ali'i* as I said means "royal." There is a plaque in front of Hapaiali'i Heiau that reads: *Literally translated means "elevated chiefs." A heiau, or temple, is a pre-Christian place of worship. Its age has been recorded as prehistoric. It is said that this heiau was built by a Ma'a, a kahuna (priest) of Maui, who left for Kaua'i later. Others say that it was built by Kamehameha about 1782 after the battle of Moku'ohai, and that Hewahewa was its priest. It was also said that the ali'i women would hanau or give birth at this heiau to instill the great mana or spiritual power within their child.*

You can either cross the old bridge or walk on the stone across the tide pool at low tide. You'll find Ke'eku Heiau, the site of the execution of the king and his dogs mentioned earlier, immediately at the south end of the bridge. Currently under reconstruction, Ke'eku Heiau is one of the most venerated religious sites in Hawaii because of its legendary associations with the 16th century wars between Hawaii Island and Maui.

At low tide in front of Ke'eku Heiau, you can see the petroglyphs carved into the rocks.

South of the heiau once stood the 462 room Kona Lagoon Hotel, closed since 1988. It was said to be cursed as it was built upon sacred *aina*, sacred land. It was torn down in 2004, in order to restore historic sites. For quite a few years, it was a ghost hotel. If you were brave enough, you could enter its empty dilapidated halls and wander around among the vacant rooms. Truly eerie!

If you can do the half-mile walk along Ali'i Drive from Kahalu'u Beach to the Surf and Racket club, you can walk in and explore the remains of the astounding king's palace, Lonoikamakakahiki. Built by Umi, one of Hawaii's greatest kings over 500 years ago, it was inhabited by other great kings, including Kamehameha. It was here that Kalanio'pu'u, king of Hawaii, fled to hide from British sailors bent on vengeance after the death of Captain Cook in Kealakekua.

After all this exploration, you might get back before the shaved-ice wagon leaves Kahalu'u Beach for the day. Stick around for sunset; usually, sunsets are spectacular here. Most people go home; you may get the beach all to yourself. If you're up to it, this is also a good time for one last dip in the sea before dark.

#16
Kauna'oa Beach
(Mauna Kea Beach)

Getting there: Take Highway 19 north from Kona. Kauna'oa Beach is approximately 32 miles north of Kailua-Kona in the Kohala resort area, just south of Kawaihae. Go past Hapuna Beach and turn left just **past mile-marker 69**. Follow the road to the end of the road for public access and limited parking: only 30 "public" cars are allowed at any one time, so it is best to come early, before 9:00 a.m. Once all the parking passes are issued, you'll have to wait for someone to leave the beach before you can enter to park. You can get a free pass and map from the security office at the entrance of the hotel. Visitors can stay at the beach for as long as they want. Well, I mean, you can't camp there, but you can stay through the evening. If you're staying at the Mauna Kea or its nearby sister resort, Hapuna Beach Prince Hotel, of course, you have full access to the beach and parking isn't a problem. You can also hike here along the one-mile shoreline trail from the north end of Hapuna Beach, which is a lovely hike.

Oh the beautiful Mauna Kea Beach and hotel. They go together in my mind with my first magical days in Hawaii and that fresh, astonished feeling of having found paradise! Kauna'oa was the first beach on the Big Island I ever visited. I had come to Hilo to study art and tropical horticulture at the university; a new friend offered to take me to a "good" beach. He said the east side beaches were "crap." I remember the shock I got when we drove through Waimea—it was rainy, dark, and cold and people were wearing parkas! Not rain parkas, snow parkas!

"But this is supposed to be Hawaii," I exclaimed! "I came to Hawaii for sun and beach and turquoise water and swaying palm trees and full moons like vanilla orbs!."

My friend laughed mischievously.

Then we rounded Waimea town and headed back south, stopping at the Mauna Kea. And there it was, the beach of my tropical dreams.

Visually stunning, it was perfect. With gleaming white sands, it looked like a crescent moon fallen to earth. No wonder Laurance Rockefeller chose this site for the luxury Hawaiian hotel he envisioned. (He was quoted as saying, "Every great beach deserves a great hotel.") When he first saw it, it was a beach on a desolate hillside of barren lava rock, surrounded by thorny kiawe bushes. In his mind's eye, he saw the jewel of a possibility—an elegant secluded resort blending into the environment, with perfect sunshine, fine white sand, calm trade winds, and turquoise waters, crowned with a view of the majestic and sometimes snow-capped 14,000 feet high Mauna Kea volcano.

No wonder the ali'i came here to relax and play in the surf!

The land above the bay is owned by Parker Ranch. In 1960, the governor of the new state of

Hawaii invited Rockefeller for a visit, and Rockefeller was invited to swim in the bay. Plans for its "development" began in 1961. As part of the "deal," what ever went down, the State agreed to pave Queen Ka'ahumanu Highway to the resort and build the Kona Airport. Remember, back in those days, the highway didn't exist. Nothing existed out here; it was miles and miles of frozen black lava.

Rockefeller in turn bought the nearby land of Pu'ukohala Heiau and donated it for a National Historical Park. The original plan for the hotel was to build a series of small cottages, but ultimately this plan was scrapped, and instead, one of the most elegant five-star hotels of its time opened in 1965.

In 1973 a lawsuit was filed to allow public access to the beach, and after seven years of litigation, an agreement was reached to allow public access and a limited amount of parking for the public. Also the trails along the shoreline were opened to the public. This set the important precedent for public access to all the beaches in Hawaii, and this is why you and I can swim, surf and snorkel on beaches such as this one, which otherwise would be restricted to the One Per Cent.

In the large earthquake of 2006, the Mauna Kea experienced extensive damage, and was closed for renovation until it reopened in 2009.

Kauna'oa is one of the most beautiful beaches on the island. The water here is perfect. The gentle gradual slope of the cove, which has a natural rock reef that offers protection from the surf, provides excellent swimming conditions most all year round. The waves are generally perfect for body boarding and boogie boarding. One good thing about having the hotel here and limiting public parking is that the beach is never too crowded.

Stretching luxuriously for a half mile, most of the bay is sandy-bottomed and less than ten feet deep, making for easy and safe snorkeling for beginners. The powdery white sand stretches far out into the water, making it easy to enter.

There are two coral reefs. The coral reefs extend 800 meters in length. On the southern end, which is generally the calmest and most suitable for children and novice swimmers, there is a great snorkeling area among the rocks. Waves here are gentler than at next-door Hapuna Beach.

On the right side, the north end, nearest the hotel, you can swim along the rocky ledge which is where you'll see the most fish, since the rocks and coral provide food and shelter for them.

If you like to swim long distances, like I do, this is probably the best beach on the island for that. You can swim parallel to the beach without getting far from shore, just like in an Olympic pool. Paddle boarding and kayaking are also good here.

In winter, there can be pounding shore breaks and rip currents: be alert. Kauna'oa Beach has bathrooms and showers, really nice ones for the public, but there are no lifeguards on duty. Occasionally sharks enter the bay (*he he*), and sometimes oodles of tiny jellyfish. If you see posted warnings, do not enter the water.

The Mauna Kea Hotel is itself part of the reason I love to come here. The staff is warm and inviting, to the locals as well as to its guests. I have always encountered real aloha spirit here, unlike at some of the other 5-star hotels which have usurped the beaches along the golden coast. The grounds of the hotel are lovely. There are beachfront outlets to rent snorkel and diving gear, and a number of eateries to choose from. By the way, the Sunday all-you-can eat brunch, is the best on the Island, as is their Christmas, Easter, and New Year's Day brunch. Try the melt in your mouth crème brulee. It's the absolute best I have ever tasted. (I wasn't paid to say this.)

If you decide to do more than swim and then sunbathe for a long while (you may *not* want to do anything else; for some reason, sunbathing here is special), you might want to get up a game of volleyball. The hotel has a volleyball court, and the public is allowed to enjoy it. Or you just might want to sit in the shade of the many shade trees and read a good book.

Or, if you want, you can pick up the Ala Kekaha Kai Trail. You can hike from here all the way to Spencer Beach Part, to the north, or south to Hapuna. If you hike north, you will find two more white sand small beaches, Waiulaula Beach and Mau'umae Beach.

Sunsets can be spectacular here, as the beach faces due west. This is a popular time for wedding ceremonies on the beach. How lovely to watch a beautiful bride in white getting married. High heels in the sand?

After sunset, head over to Manta Ray Point. The hotel shines floodlights into the water to attract plankton, tiny crustaceans called krill. Why? Because plankton, *hahalua* in Hawaiian, is the favorite food of manta rays. More often than not, the manta rays, with wingspans up to thirty feet (!), can easily be seen in the clear water, undulating, gliding in slow motion—gentle giants slowly somersaulting and turning with incredible grace.

I reserve Mauna Kea for really special occasions, when I really want to treat myself, or when I want to get back into touch with that special feeling I had when I first arrived in the Islands. I go early, take my gear, snorkel and fins, etc. and also a sundress and sandals, get my "public parking spot," and spend the day on the beach.

In the late afternoon, I shower and change, "put on the dog," so to speak, and then head for the hotel, where I love to stroll and just look at the 1600 piece museum quality Pacific and Asian art collection gathered by Mr. Rockefeller. He was a great collector, and this collection was put together with the geography of the Pacific Rim and spirituality in mind.

My favorite is the 7th Century granite figure of the Buddha meditating at the top of the grand staircase. I never see this but I get chills. There are also really fine boutiques and art galleries to explore, all out of my price range, of course, but I can look, can't I? I also really enjoy the koi ponds.

For the all around primo Hawaii experience, don't miss making a day of it at this wonderful beach.

#17
Road to the Sea Black Sand Beach
(Kaupua'a Beach)

Getting there: A lot of the adventure of this beach is getting there! A lot of it is in the wildness of this desolate, lava encrusted no-man's land.

Be forewarned: **there are *no* services of any kind.** You must bring everything you need, and especially lots of water. There is little shade and it's very hot and dry. Take lots of water and good hiking shoes. This is almost entirely a'a lava, the sharp kind.

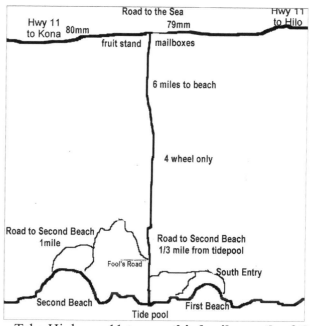

Take Highway 11 to **one-third mile north of the 79-marker,** where there is a gravel road on the makai (ocean) side of the road. This is Road to the Sea. There is a colorful but usually closed fruit stand on the corner and a boat near the fruit stand. This bouncy, rutted road, which might make you appreciate the old pioneers who headed west in wagon trains, drops along a nearly straight line 1500 feet down to the sea. It traverses a little more than six miles of desolate aʻa lava from an old Mauna Loa eruption. Turn down the gravel road; this is the start of a rugged, partly **4-wheel road** that will lead down to the ocean and a number of secluded green sand beaches with trails, fishing, swimming and surfing spots.

Plan for *at least* 45 minutes to get down the road. The first beach is at the end of the road.

The road is very rough in spots, to say the least; a regular car can do the first three miles, but a 4-wheel is a must for the remainder half of the road. You could also park your car and walk the last three miles.

You will see signs saying that the road is private. This means it is not maintained by the county; the road is maintained by the handful of people who live on it. Believe it or not, people have elected to live in this incredibly barren landscape made up of only lava rock for as far as you can see. These hardy souls live off the grid and supply their own electricity through solar power and get their water from water catchment. Those round tanks you see are water catchment tanks. This road is their lifeline. Be respectful; don't tear down it as fast as you can go. Just like the ancient people of Ka'u, who were known for disposing of chiefs they didn't like, the people of Ka'u are known to take the law into their own hands. So, once again, be respectful!

As you drive by, you are looking at the frozen lava flow of the most recent flow of 1908, as well as older flows. Watch on the right. You will sometimes see a *mulliwai*, a channel that funneled lava toward the sea. The large round boulders you see are pieces of lava that rolled down, getting bigger and bigger, just like a snowball rolling down a hill.

Before you reach the halfway mark, look toward the right for "Face Rock," an a'a lava boulder that stands as sentinel over the road. He'll be watching to see how you respect his road!

At about the 3-mile point, the road jags to the right. Here is where you have to walk if you don't have 4-wheel. You will see a gated road on the left. Keep on Road to the Sea.

Approaching the end of Road to the Sea, the road becomes rougher and rougher and then you come to a large loop at the end. You can take the loop to the left and park or you can keep driving down behind a dune to another spot. Both spots are green sand beaches. This rocky shoreline land is a rugged and wild, flat tidal shelf, laced with tide pools, patches of green sand, and coral storm beaches.

Once, long ago, there was a village here, Keawaiki. Because of the presence of at last one brackish well here, possibly more, the people could survive in an area that had a rich reef for fishing and shelter along the bluffs. Here also was once an ancient temple. It was all destroyed by an eruption in 1859. You may see cars parked here, and possibly some campers, but please, **do not drive on the sand**, even though others do, as you will be destroying the eggs of the rare and endangered hawksbill turtle.

To the locals of Ka'u, this is Half-Moon Bay, but Humuhumu Point is the official name. *Humuhumu* means "to fit pieces together" and probably refers to the triggerfish, Humuhumunukunukuapua'a (one of the longest names in the Hawaiian language). Can you say it? *Hu-mu-hu-mu-nu-ku-nu-ku-a-pu-a-a.* Poetical, isn't it? *Apua'a* means "pig" and *nukunuku* means "small snout," but locals usually just call the fish a "Humuhumu."

The two imposing littoral cones in the distance are *Na Pu'u a Pele* at Keawaiki, the hill of Pele at Keawaiki, also sometimes called Pele's Breasts.

Littoral means shoreline. In this case, the cones here were built of lava fragments from a lava flow pouring into the sea. Lava entering the ocean heated and boiled the seawater, generating steam explosions that hurled tephra, volcanic fragments of lava and rock, onto the shore. As the various tephra accumulated on the shoreline, a well-developed cone was created.

There is a legend, of course, about the Na Pu'u a Pele.

The chiefs of the area had fallen in love with a beautiful, mysterious girl who sometimes visited their villages, but because she had a fiery temper, they began to suspect that she was Pele, the goddess of the volcano. Spurning her therefore, she became enraged and really gave them a dose of her temper. Talk about a woman's unrequited love! She turned into a wrathful old woman who stomped the ground with her feet, causing earthquakes to sweep the land of Kahuku, and raging lava rivers to break out in fiery floods. The terrified chiefs fled to the north, but Pele created a new flow that made them turn and run back to the south. As they reached the sea, she threw her arms around them, and thus the bodies of the chief are preserved in the Na Pu'u a Pele, in the breasts of Pele.

There are some other beaches tucked along the coast within walking distance; you'll see rough trails.

Did I say green sand beach? Yes! This is not *The* Green Sand Beach, which we will visit later on, but one of several beaches in this area with green sands. For years, the Big Island, which has fewer sand beaches per mile of shoreline than any of the other major islands, was not renowned for its great beaches. Many were unknown because of a lack of paved roads and lack of information about where to find them, but the Big Island does possess some of the most unique and intriguing stretches of sand in all of Hawaii.

The green comes from olivine crystals, a form of semi-precious gemstone called peridot, that are created during the course of volcanic formation. The green sand beaches of Hawaii are a few of only a few such beaches in the whole world. For your information, Hawaii's white sand beaches are composed primarily of quartz, a colorless silicate, and seashells and calcium carbonate. Olivine is also a silicate, but mixed with added iron and magnesium. Here it is mixed with black sand; thus the color of the sand is a darker green than at *The* Green Sand Beach we will visit later.

The green sands here are a result of erosion of the littoral cones.

It is said that the old Hawaiians believed green sand to be the tears of Goddess Pele, and they used it in healing ceremonies. It's considered bad luck to take any of it, so take heed.

Swimming, surfing and snorkeling are possible here, **if you're a good swimmer**, but be careful; the shoreline drops to very deep depths very quickly and is exposed to the open sea. The Ka'u area is famous for its fierce winds as well, **so keep out of the water during heavy winds**; they can create dangerous swimming conditions. Scuba diving is good around the rocks, but stay near shore. Strong undercurrents and riptides occur here during high surf. **Close supervision of children is a must.**

Further south, you might see some fisher folk; nearby is a tide pool where you can take a dip. If the surf is big, waves break over the rocks and the spray is quite refreshing.

It's possible you might find evidence of some of the wild local animals, the biggest two-footed ones on the Island—this beach is the location of neighborhood "full moon parties." Yes, you know the kind—howling at the moon, mad-dancing around the fire, smoking weird stuff, etc. If you want to be kind and show your appreciation to Mother Earth, you might pick up a little of any litter you find and cart it out.

This is also a popular fishing beach, and you might get some wonderful photos of fisher folk doing their thing.

'Awili Point, larger and longer than Humuhumu, is just to the north. Steep and narrow at its eastern end, it gets wider at the western end. Swimming conditions are the same as at Humuhumu. It is here that ulua fishing has become very popular with fisher folk in the last few years.

Just behind 'Awili Point, you can find an a'a lava trail that climbs to the summits of the littoral cones, the Na Pu'u a Pele. The trail then leads back down to Keawaiki and intersects with the shoreline trail going back to 'Awili.

Climb to the top of Pele's Breast—the 360-degree view is magnificent! You can get a pretty good idea of the immensity of the lava flows from Mauna Loa.

This flow, the "Hapaimanu" flow, is one of the largest single flows on the lower Southwest Rift Zone, and covers approximately 100 square kilometers of area, from Manuka Bay to the north to Humuhumu Point to the south. It occurred about 240 years ago, about 1660.

Geological mapping gives credence to the legend of Pele recounted above. There is indeed an older southern flow; refugees who fled from the flow toward the north would have in fact been turned back by the later northern flow, just as the legend recounts. The stamping of Pele's feet would have been the earthquakes that preceded the eruption.

In the latest flow of 1908, the source of the eruption, which has not been exactly located, was about at the 8500 feet elevation. Small branches flowed east and west but the main flow soon invaded the area occupied by a flow of 1887, and crossed the Road to the Sea, which was a government road at that time. The western flow then diverted, forming what is called the Manuka flow, and came down with great speed and force, as recorded by eyewitnesses. The division of the flow prevented either branch from reaching the sea, as earlier flows had.

The entire Ocean View Estates subdivision is located on this flow; its source vents are directly above the subdivision, between 5400 and 6400 feet elevation. Geologists have shown that 15 eruptions have occurred here in the last 1500 years.

Yes, that's right. A flow about once every 100 years. It's been a little more than 100 years since the last flow.

Sometimes you just have to shake your head and wonder at humankind's audacity, don't you?

Standing on top of Pele's Breast, looking back toward the great Mauna Loa, the second biggest mountain in the solar system (the largest is on Mars), and one of the world's most active volcanoes, perhaps you can get a small glimpse of Pele's awesome power, and the puniness of mankind.

#18
La'aloa
(Magic Sands, Disappearing Sands, White Sands)

Getting there: The address is 77-6470 Ali'i Drive, just north of **mile-marker four**, in Kailua. No need for a map, you will spot it *because* of all the activity around it. A conflux of happy joggers, surfers, skate boarders, boogie boarders and beautiful young wahines in thong bikinis may alert you to the precise spot. Oodles of kids come to the beach on their skateboards carrying their surf and body boards. Look for smiles and laughter.

You can sometimes park on the road, (even though there are "no parking" signs). You can also hop on the shuttle bus. It cost one dollar; you must have correct change.

La'aloa means "very sacred" in Hawaiian, and like this entire coast bordering Ali'i Drive in Kailua-Kona, La'aloa was a site of residences and temple grounds of the Hawaiian royalty. Most people now refer to it as "Magic Sands" or "Disappearing Sands," or less often as "White Sands." It gets its name "Magic" and "Disappearing" because during most of the summer and fall, it is a beautiful, white sand beach, but in winter and spring, violent storms take the sand out to sea, leaving an exposed rocky terrace. With the return of summer currents, the sands return, like magic! You know the saying, "Magic happens!" In even just one day, the sands can be there and the next day gone, and vice versa.

In the very heart of touristy Kailua-Kona, this is a lot of people's favorite beach. Why? Because it's a happy, happening beach—everyone's happy and there's lots happening! All *kine* (that's Hawaiian for "all kind of") people come here; you'll see bronzed surfers, hippies from the sixties, locals, snow bunnies, blue-haired old ladies, jet setters...all kine!

This is one, if not *the* best body boarding beaches in Hawaii, even better than Hapuna, because of the never-ending wave action that funnels the waves from the open sea—one of the best, if you know what you are doing. Magic Sands is known by another name at Kona Community Hospital—"Tragic Sands," because of the number of people hurt or paralyzed due to the violent shore break. Not kidding!

Don't get tricked by a calm *looking* beach here—waves, like the sand, appear like magic. Magic happens! Even in summer, the lifeguards make rescues almost every day. During the winter, the problems here increase astronomically as the wave power dramatically increases as well. Best thing to do, if you are going in the water, is to **ask the lifeguards if it is safe and if so, where to go and what to look out for.** I know, I know—you don't want to look like a dorky tourist, but just act casual, like you're just talking story. Better safe than sorry. Sometimes it's better to just play in the surf or wade.

Always obey the Hawaiian maxim, "Never turn your back on the sea," especially at Magic Sands. There are almost always moderately high-waves, and often, curling waves. Big Kahuna roller waves, rogue waves turning up when you least expect them, happen, just like "magic happens," though mostly in winter, unless there is a storm.

In winter, Magic Sands explodes. That's when the local surfing pros wait for the ten feet plus *bomboras*. What's a bombora? That's surfer talk for an area of large sea waves breaking over a shallow area such as a submerged rock shelf, reef or sand bank. As the wave passes over the shallow area, its shape is steepened and raised, creating a localized wave formation. Only very experienced surfers should take on bomboras—they can pose a significant hazard even in good weather, as a bombora may not always be identifiable.

With all that said, on calmer days, even when the shoreline is rocky, the sea floor is smooth sand, making this a great place to swim or wade. Try the left side of the beach for boogie boarding and swimming. You might want reef slippers.

But even if you don't go in the water, this is a great place to take a beach chair and watch the action. You'll see some real talent here! There are lots of towering coconut trees for shade (Always look up before settling under a coconut tree; coconuts can kill! A coconut palm tree commonly reaches 25 meters in height, a coconut can weigh four pounds or more, and a four-pound coconut falling 25 meters would have a velocity of 80 kilometers per hour on impact and a force of as much as 1,000 kilograms. How's that for some scientific statistics? Be reassured, though. In most county parks, the coconut trees are trimmed regularly. Still, look!).

Get to the beach before 7 a.m. before anyone else arrives, for quiet meditation time. You might take some breadcrumbs for the gentle little zebra doves that abound here; they are very tame and will eat out of your hand. Listen to their soothing coos. I always associate that sweet sound with Hawaii.

There are always lifeguards on duty here, plus showers, bathrooms, and volleyball net. Volleyball is big on this beach, and you'll see some great skill. If you want to play, just ask.

During low surf, snorkeling is great. Head around the southern point and the rocks below. If you dive, the small bay just south of the parking lot at La'aloa has beautiful coral gardens and really wild topography, with caves and canyons, plus a great variety of reef fish. Snorkeling is good here too, and you might see dolphins. Wear reef shoes to get over the stony beach.

Makai (toward the sea) of the parking lot is Haukalua Heiau, a very sacred temple site, roughly 800 years old. It was dismantled to build the parking lot! **Please do not wander around it**; the locals are highly protective of what remains of it.

Where the restrooms stand is the original site of Saint Peter's Church, the Little Blue Church, which is now at Kahalu'u Beach. It was placed on poles and moved by donkeys before Ali'i Drive was paved in 1912.

If you hit Magic Sands when the sands have disappeared, you can always head down the road to Kahalu'u.

#19
Pololu Valley Beach
(Long Spear Beach)

Getting there: (Sixty–two miles from Kona). Getting there is a lot of the fun. On the way you can stop in the quaint little towns of Hawi and Kapa'au. The road continues on over single-lane bridges, passing old plantation-style homes. You may even get a view of Maui on a clear day.

The north end of the Big Island, Kohala, is one of the least explored areas of this beautiful island. The drive to Pololu is beautiful and makes a wonderful day excursion.

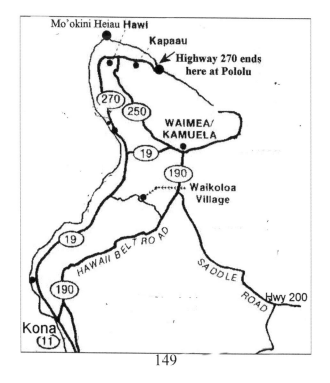

Take Highway 19 from Kailua-Kona to Kawaihae, and then take Highway 270. This is the most scenic route. *(You can also take Highway 250 from Waimea town, where you can either intersect Highway 270 at Hawi or Kapa'au. See the map). You'll pass Lapakahi State Historical Park, the birthplace of King Kamehameha I, and at the very northern tip of the island, Mo'okini Heiau. For the Heiau, which I recommend, look for mile-marker 20 and turn left at the 'Upolu Airport. From there, take the dirt road to the left that leads to the heiau. If there have been heavy rains, don't try it; the road may be impassible, unless you have four-wheel drive.

Approximately two miles from the airport, you will come to Mo'okini Heiau. *Mo'okini* means "many lineages" and is said to refer to the large reptile, or dragon, goddesses of very ancient times. This is a luakini temple, a temple where people were put to death (*luakini* means "many graves"); it was erected about 480 A.D. and is the largest temple in Hawaii. It was dedicated to Ku, the Hawaiian god of war. The stones from which it is built were passed hand over hand from the Pololu Valley, more than 14 miles away, by a living chain of men In one night! An incredible feat, which you will appreciate more when you see Pololu Valley.

The large lava slab with the dip in it in front of the heiau is the Papanui Oleka, where sacrifices were made—people were put to death to feed the gods. You might find the energy a bit eerie and unsettling. Interestingly, there is a living kahuna who presides over and protects this ancient temple of sacrifice. She is a priestess who was once a police sergeant. She claims to trace her ancestry back to ancient temples in Fiji, India, and the Persian Gulf.

The exact birthplace of King Kamehameha I is a few hundred yards away. It is called Kamehameha Akahi Aina Hanau. It's believed by many that he was born in 1758, when Halley's Comet passed overhead.

After visiting the heiau, retrace the road. Then you'll drive through the little village of **Hawi**, once a bustling sugar town, with its quaint shops. The Bamboo Restaurant is considered one of the best places to eat on the Island, by the way. Continue on past Kapa'au, where you can see the famous statue of King Kamehameha.

Take Highway 270 east from Kapa'au to the end of the road. A jaw-dropping view appears quite unexpectedly when the road comes around a turn and the valley comes into sight. The beach is located below the Pololu Lookout at mile-marker 28.

It's impossible to see into the valley and its beach from the lookout itself. You have to hike at least halfway down in order to look back up into the valley and down into the beach.

There are **no facilities, no lifeguards** and little roadside parking. Make sure to bring insect repellent, as the area tends to attract mosquitoes. Big ones! You'll need about a liter of water per person. Children can do this hike, depending on the children. Travelers with young children should keep them close if there has been a recent rainfall—there can be loose rocks, so use caution. I've seen very small children hiking as well as parents backpacking babies. Depends on your level of fitness!

This is a wonderful place for a memorable tropical picnic. It is also one of the last places on the Big Island to wilderness camp.

What a change in scenery from the dry volcanic deserts along the coast to the lush forests and massive cliffs of North Kohala! Spectacular and mysterious, Pololu Valley Beach provides an incredible view of the rugged Kohala coastline and mountains and is one of the most photographed places of the Big Island— its majesty has graced the cover of numerous magazines, books, and travelogues umpteen times. The beach itself is a steep 400 feet down, and can only be reached after a strenuous 25 minute or so hike from the lookout area down steep steps on a zigzagging dirt path. Be especially careful if the ground is wet.

Worth the every breath it takes to hike back up! And, it will give you a deep appreciation of how those stones for Mo'okini Heiau were obtained.

Allow at least two hours, and maybe three, for the hike down and back up. The moderately-difficult trail has some steps carved into the path, and obvious rocks to step on, and is about four miles long; it descends nearly 1000 feet, traversing the Pololu stream at times, which can be trickling or more rapid, but at any rate, not too difficult to cross. The trail meanders through groves of ironwood and hau trees and across marchlands. Be sure you have your camera—there are stunning views of waterfalls and the sea cliffs dropping dramatically down into the water.

Pololu is the furthest west of the seven valleys at the northern end of the Big Island. Once it was renowned for its *kalo* (taro), which was a particular variety (*kalo pololu*) with crimson stems; the valley was at one time densely populated by wet taro farmers. Taro farming was complemented by rice farming in the 1800's, but fear of tsunamis, and the building of the Kohala ditch, which diverted water from the Honokane Valley to the sugarcane fields of the North Kohala district, led the Hawaiians to abandon these valleys.

During World War II, the valley was used by the military to practice amphibious operations, and metal-landing tracks can still be found down here.

Water activities are not recommended at this beach due to the strong currents and high surf conditions; the channel here between the Big Island and Maui is said to have the highest discharge of water in the world; this generates extremely fast ocean currents and strong rip tides. Some people do brave the rough surf and go for a swim at this beach, but use extreme caution, especially in winter. I've heard reports of people scuba diving here, but I don't advise it, due to the above facts.

If you do swim, or camp on the beach, be on guard for Portuguese Man-o-War. Carried in by the tide, they are very beautiful translucent shades of blue; they pack a powerful sting that can temporarily paralyze their victim. If one should wrap its tentacles around you, don't try to rub them off with sand; this rubs the poison into the skin. The best remedy is to pee on them. If severe pain sets in, head for the hospital.

Views from the beach are incredible. Surrounded by giant walled sea cliffs, with a meandering stream winding through the middle of the valley, the emerald-green landscape with its little waterfalls will feel like an enchanted forest.

Once you are down in the valley, you can sit on a piece of driftwood and allow yourself to be mesmerized by the sucking, popping sounds of waves being pulled back over the round melon-sized lava rocks at the far end of the beach. This is a great place to meditate. As a matter of interest, is said that, in olden days, this valley was a place where a chanter could test his voice against the wind and the waves.

You will see huge rope swings that hang from the trees and bridges that look like an ancient playground —the locals have built these from old tires and beach flotsam. You're likely to find other interesting flotsam here. There are numerous fire pits as well.

Trails lead just off the beach into the woods. Follow the trail up the opposite side of the valley for splendid views into the back of the valley. You may be tempted to cut out across the interior of Pololu; you'll quickly find out it's better to stick to the trail— off-trail is boggy and hard going.

Pololu is the starting point for over 40 miles of interconnecting tails through these northern valleys. Trails in this area are steep, unmaintained, and crumbling, and in the rain are frequently quite slick, so caution is advised, particularly on hill slopes, when trails may turn into streambeds and hillsides into waterfalls.

If you plan to do more extensive hiking, you should know that stream water in the valleys is infected with leptospirosis bacteria. Leptospirosis can kill. Do not drink it or go into it with open sores. Bring plenty of water and you might want rain gear; there can be rainsqualls, big or little, coming off the sea.

Following the trail past the gate along the ridge, there are even more wonderful views—after about one and a half miles you will come to a spectacular view of the next valley over, Honokane Nui. The trail continues down into that valley.

From here the trails are challenging; you will need a topographical map minimum and a GPS is recommended. The land beyond Pololu Valley is privately owned; you must get an access permit from the Surety Kohala Company, which has an office next to the Hawi Post Office. Call 808-889-6257 for additional information. You have to sign a waiver. They recommend you hike with someone who knows the area. Emergency crews evacuate on average two or three hiking or hunting groups a month.

I've never done it, I can't find anyone to hike it with me, but it's possible to hike through all seven valleys all the way to Waipi'o. That means about fifteen miles traversing 14 canyons and fording numerous streams, a rigorous journey of several days.

The trail back out of Pololu will probably seem longer and steeper than was the trail down—to be expected. Take your time, and enjoy the hike up. It is well worth every breath!

#20
Keawaiki Beach, the Golden Ponds, Pueo Bay and Weliweli Point

Getting to Keawaiki: Few people know how to find Keawaiki, the Golden Ponds, Pueo Bay, and Weliweli Point. * (Do not confuse this Keawaiki with the one down south in Ka'u). There are two ways to get there.

(1) Drive north on Highway 19, about 20 miles, to just after **mile-marker 79** and park near the boulders, which block the road-turned-into-trail. From here, it's a moderately difficult hiking trail along a gravel, and then lava road, towards the ocean. You will pass some large boulders, and then pass a gate. When the road intersects the fence, take the smaller trail to the right. There will be a barbed wire fence along the trail all the way to the beach. It's a little more than four miles round trip. No facilities, of course. When the trail meets the coast, you have arrived at Keawaiki Bay. For directions to Pueo Bay and Weliweli, see just below.

(2) The second way to get here is to simply hike **south** from Anaeho'omalu Beach along the King's Trail. From Kona take Highway 19 north toward the Kohala resort area. Make a left turn at **mile-marker 76**. Turn left again at the road across from the Kings' Shops. Beach parking is available at the end of this road. It's about a two-mile hike southward to Weliweli Point from here.

In this section, I will describing the first directions from mile-marker 79, hiking toward the **north**.

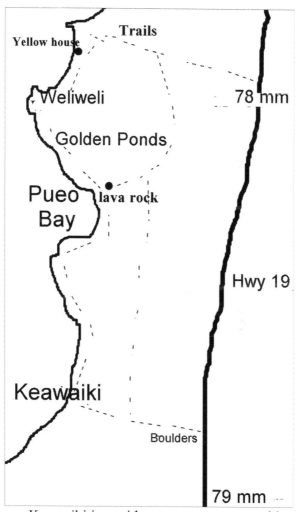

Keawaiki is a wide, steep, very unusual beach. What makes it so unusual? It is both a black and white sand beach! Perhaps the only one like it in the world! Created when Mauna Loa erupted in 1859, the north part of the beach is black from the lava flow, while the south part of the beach, untouched by the lava, is white. It's been a century and a half since that eruption; the sands are slowly mixing, as wave action carries them in and out, but as of yet, they have not mixed totally together.

Keawaiki is an exposed beach and reef break familiar to avid surfers. When good waves are happening, there can be a small crowd, though most of the crowd is in the water; otherwise, you are likely to have it all to yourself. Snorkeling is good on the south side, where the sand is predominantly white and the reef offers protection; this area is rich in many varieties of tropical fish. You'll find some shade from the fierce heat. The floor here is shallow and rocky. Be aware of riptides and the presence of sharks (*he he*), and in winter especially, wave action can become dangerously rough. If you walk south of the white sand, you can explore a number of beautiful tide pools. You might want to take reef slippers for safer hiking. Notice the salt deposits from evaporated seawater—you might also see wild goats that come here to lick the salt.

If you hike north of Keawaiki, you are heading toward the lovely **Pueo Bay,** with its large black and white pebbles. It was formed by the 1859 Mauna Loa lava flow. *Pueo* mean "owl" and the owl is an *aumakua*, a guardian spirit, of many Hawaiian families. Swimming is usually pretty good here in the calm water and snorkeling also; there are many freshwaters springs so you can encounter interesting underwater riffs and distortions in the current. There isn't any shade so be prepared with a hat. Surfing can be good here when waves are up.

From here, you can hike back to the highway—watch for the big lava rock, the trail is to the right. Or, you can hike on north to Weliweli via the coral-marked trail.

The tip of land to the north is **Weliweli Point**. Snorkeling and diving is rewarding but remember—you are in the open ocean. Be cautious of currents. You can hike on toward the house you see on the point; there is a trail that picks up on the other side of it that you can follow back to the highway; you'll end up about mile-marker 78. Or you can retrace your steps. You may have beautiful views of Kohala Mountain and Haleakula on Maui from Weliweli.

Take a little time and look closely at the a'a lava here; you will see large crystals of olivine. These are products of the volcanic eruption. Though there is no green sand beach here, there could be one day as the crystals are broken down by wave action. More about this in the section on Green Sands Beach.

When you are behind Pueo Bay, look for a large *ahu* (cairn) of white coral. This marks the way to the **Golden Ponds**. You can easily spot them because they are surrounded by the only vegetation in this barren land, a few hala trees.

These twin golden ponds owe their beautiful hue to the algae growing in them. Enjoy the ponds, but tread lightly—they support a very delicate ecosystem.

All along here you will see the remains of ancient dwellings and heiau. Do not disturb them by removing any stones or climbing on them.

A point of romantic interest is that a large parcel of Keawaiki was once owned by Francis I'i Brown, a direct descendent of John Papa I'i, a distinguished and highborn native Hawaiian historian. Brown was a businessman, champion golfer and legislator during the early and mid-twentieth century. He acquired the estate at Keawaiki during the late 1920's. He was rumored to have thrown wild parties here, or at least lavish entertainments, with celebrities such as Bob Hope and Babe Ruth. At that time, the estate was accessible only by water.

Interestingly, he built a compound that seems to have been modeled somewhat like the ancient royal compounds, including a fishpond, surrounded by residences and a coconut grove. In the center of the pond was a pavilion, a tiny bedroom, made for Winona Love, his half-English, half-Hawaiian sweetheart, one of the most beautiful and beloved hula dancers of her time.

There are numerous trails to make your way back to the car or Keawaiki Beach. You can ponder the history and wild beauty of this place all the way back.

#21
Anaeho'omalu Bay
(A-Bay, Waikoloa Beach)

Getting there: This beach, known to locals as A-Bay, is on the ocean side of Waikoloa Resort (about 24.5 miles from Kona). Take Highway 19 north from Kona toward the Kohala Resort Area. Turn left at **mile-marker 76**, which is Waikoloa Beach Drive. Turn left at the road across from the Kings' Shops. Take a left after you pass the Queen's Marketplace and continue to the left through the gate. Parking for the beach is at the end of this road and is free. At the south end of the Bay, there is a paved path. The park is open from 7 a.m. to 8 p.m., after which the gates are locked. There are restrooms and showers at the beginning of the path.

A-Bay is sometimes an alternative to the busier beaches along the Kohala Coast. A palm-fringed shallow water bay, it's famous for its sunsets, snorkeling and ancient fishponds. It offers fairly good swimming year around, due to the protection from the offshore reef. The coarse white sand contains fine particles of volcanic ash.

The water is very shallow and can be at times murky for some reason. But the lovely bay with so many palm trees is still good for a great full day at the beach. You might even see a rare Hawaiian monk seal.

This is a kind of "entertainment" beach and a good beach for family activities. A very popular windsurfing location, the Waikoloa Beach Resort offers glass bottom boat rides (pretty cool! With visibility to 200 feet!) and outrigger canoeing (you can get lessons) and rents kayaks and canoes. The bay itself, being very shallow, is a boat mooring spot; some boats offer area cruises, including sailing and diving charters, and windsurfing rentals and lessons. You can also rent beach umbrellas, snorkeling gear, and beach chairs. Deep-sea fishing charters, as well as dolphin and whale watching tours are offered. You can take surfing lessons too.

Just about everything having to do with water, you can do here.

Do be aware that there are no lifeguards.

This is also the location of the Lava Man Triathlon, one of the qualifying events for the world famous Iron Man Triathlon.

The historical Ala Ali'i King's Trail runs along the coast and there is a very large petroglyph field, rock shelter and ancient sites scattered through the area. If you follow the trail south to Kapalaoa Beach, you will find the wild-looking, usually uninhabited little beach with golden sand and its good snorkeling on the south side. You can actually follow this trail all the way to Pueo Bay and Keawaiki Beach, described earlier. If you follow the trail north, you will arrive at the Hilton Waikoloa resort. It meanders over lava, coral, and around numerous tide pools. You'll need shoes to traverse the lava and coral path. This makes a great sunset walk.

Follow the signs through the Kings' Shops to the large petroglyph field, which is actually in the center of the golf course! You can pick up a self-guided tour brochure in the mall. Viewing is best early in the morning or around sunset, when the angle of the sun is low. Remember—do not disturb the petroglyphs by making rubbings or in other ways.

A big plus that you won't find at other beaches is that you can sometimes find seashells here. Between the sandy beach and the petroglyph field is a rocky area where a variety of cowry and conch shells may be washed up. Finders—keepers!

For more privacy, there is a little garden area overlooking the beach that makes for quiet sunbathing and book reading.

Early in the morning, before too many people arrive, you can see the turtles sunning themselves at the far end of the bay. They are endangered; please do not disturb them.

The hotel provides very nice showers, restrooms, and picnic tables.

There are a number of good restaurants here, including local cuisine, seafood, Chinese food—you name it, it's probably here.

Anaeho'omalu Bay gets its name from *Ana'e*, which means "mullet" and *ho'omalu*, which means "to protect" and refers to the ancient fishponds located here. Long ago, a large population resided here, due to the fishponds and drinkable water, which comes from fresh underground springs. This may have been the largest aquaculture garden in all of ancient Hawaii and was quite ingenious.

Small channels between the sea and the ponds were connected by little slatted gates, which permitted small fish to enter. Once inside, the fish gorged themselves on the algae and nutrients in the pond until they became too large to get back through the gates. When they were needed, they could easily be harvested. You can still see mullet in the ponds.

Ku'u ali'i, the southern fishpond and *Kahapapa*, the northern fishpond, are still actively maintained, although the Japanese tsunami of 2011 did extensive damage. You can see *Ku'ula pohaku* and *Hinapukui'a*, the god of fishponds and his wife, sacred stones which form part of the temple area.

Other archeological sites in the area include a *hale noa*, a traditional house where the family slept together, and a *mua*, a men's eating house. You know, of course, that back in those days, men and women could not eat together, on pain of death. In fact, it was the breaking of this kapu, when Queen Ka'ahumanu ate with her stepson, the new king, upon the death of King Kamehameha, which heralded the downfall of the old ways and religion, and made room for the new.

You might also find it interesting that in the old times, the men did the cooking. They pretty much had control over all the food. Women were not permitted to eat pork or bananas, as well as many kinds of fish.

Hurrah for Queen Kaáhumanu!

The area around the ponds makes for beautiful sunset photography.
A'ho!

#22

Ka Lae and Green Sands Beach (Papakolea, also called Mahana) at South Point

Getting there: Drive south on Hwy 11. Turn south onto South Point **Road between mile-markers 69 and 70**. There is will be a clearly marked sign. Drive 12 miles, passing sweet little farms with horses and cows grazing. You can get an idea how windy this place is by the trees; they have grown bent to the south. Those tall, white, surreal-looking structures are windmills of the Kamaoa and Pakini Nuie Wind Farms, which theoretically can provide power for 100 homes, though they are now in somewhat disrepair with fractured and missing blades—slow down or stop for a moment and listen to the sad and mournful song they sing. The road is newly paved until closer to the bottom.

See the map on the next page.

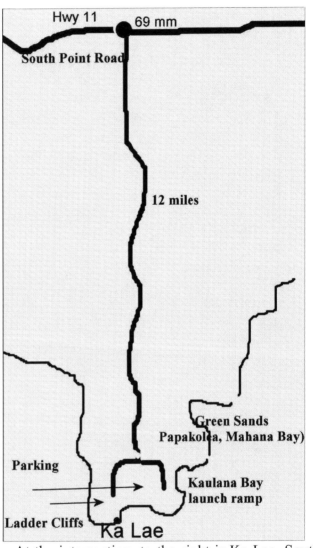

At the intersection, to the right is Ka Lae, South Point; to the left is Kaulana Bay and Green Sands. If you are up for a longer hike of it to Green Sands, go right —this leads to the destroyed boat ramp and a trail that follows the coast, *adding another two miles* to your hike to the beach. A fascinating trail. All along here you will see pre-contact archeological remains, including a heiau.

Some hardy souls, mostly local, jump from the boat hoists and climb back up via the ladders, and there are a few places where you can climb down to the water. However, **I caution against swimming or snorkeling in this area.** The ocean surge is extremely powerful.

If you go left, you come to the so-called *Visitor Center*. You might be asked for money, but keep going to the boat launch a quarter mile away and park for free. You'll come to a dirt parking lot—there will probably already be other cars there. From here it is a little more than a two-mile walk to the beach, so we're talking almost five miles round trip. You should allow at least an hour going and returning, depending on your fitness. The trail is rugged and dusty and hot over rolling tropical prairie-type terrain; make sure you have hiking shoes, not slippahs! It's impossible to get lost—you will never be out of sight of the shore. You'll see lots of rutted jeep trails; you can walk along any of them.

In addition, there are almost always locals who can navigate these trails, and will probably offer to give you a ride down and back (be sure and offer a tip; I suggest between $10 and $20 dollars; times are especially hard in this remote area), but it isn't recommended that you try to drive it in your rented SUV, unless you are a very experienced off-road driver. You will see people driving 4-wheel vehicles; however, vehicles are technically prohibited here, and besides, your rental company probably prohibits you driving here. You will also see people bottoming-out. Also, even light rains turn the trails to dangerous muck. Notice the environmental damage of all the washed out tracks. Not recommended.

When you get to the cove you are about a hundred feet above the beach on the rim of the crater —stand and peruse one of the most incredible views on the Big Island. The steep cliffs, the boulders, the colors of the sand are wild and beautiful. It was here, at **Ka Lae**, that the first Polynesians first sighted land and made landfall after voyaging for more than a month. Imagine their feelings as they looked up at majestic Mauna Loa, towering 14,000 feet above, perhaps even snow mantled. Some geologists speculate that it was erupting at the time.

Yep, from here there's nothing between you and Antarctica but the deep blue sea. This is Ka Lae.

From here, you make a steep descent down to the beach; the ground is loose and can break away so please watch your step. Look around the top rim, there is a small ladder that takes you down to natural steps in the rock. Do not try to hike down the steep face of Pu'u o Mahana, itself—the cone easily crumbles. You might see locals leaping from the cliffs into the water below, and be tempted to take this shortcut to the beach, but this is not recommended. They are experienced and know the water—you don't. Sounds tricky but young and old do make this hike.

Don't go down if the beach if the surf is up! Currents and undertows are strong and completely exposed to the open ocean!

No matter which trail you choose, this is at any rate a full day trip. You will need lots of water (keep extra water in your car), a hat, a t-shirt and probably sunscreen. Most of the time, it's hot, dry, and *really* windy. There are *no* services down by South Point, so be prepared. **Cell phones usually don't get reception.** It's best to start out early in the morning before the winds get up; don't try to make the hike in the evening or in the dark.

Please do not take the sand!

Ka Lae means "the point" and this is the southernmost point of the Big Island, and the United States. Believed to be the site of the very earliest Hawaiian settlement, there are ruins of a heiau here, and also a fishing shrine. Archeological evidence shows that people have inhabited the area since 124 A.D.

The ancient Hawaiians drilled holes in the rock ledges to moor their canoes so they could fish without being swept out to sea. This is one of Hawaii's most popular fishing spots, due to the confluence of sea currents just offshore. These currents also make this a place prone to the accumulation of marine debris, which, due to the remoteness, is not easily removed. Thus wildlife, such as monk seals and hawksbill turtles, both endangered species, are further threatened due to the possibility of entanglement in the debris.

During World War II there was a landing strip here, but it was closed in 1953. NASA once proposed a space launch here, but finally conceded that the area was too remote. Can you imagine a space shuttle being launched out of the cliffs here?

The fascinating color of the sands is due to the erosion of the littoral cinder cone Pu'u Mahana, which itself was formed by the interaction of magma and shallow groundwater over 49,000 years ago. Wave action wore away the cone, removing the lighter grains of sand made of volcanic ash, and leaving the denser olivine crystal, also known as peridot when it is of gemstone quality. This is truly a bejeweled beach.

You will hear this beach called sometimes "Mahana" after the cinder cone, and sometimes "Papakolea," after the land area here; Papakolea refers to the Pacific Golden Plover, a bird that comes here in winter.

When the ocean is calm, you can swim, snorkel, boogie board, and dive, but more often the water is rough. Remember, this is the head of an unprotected bay; at times, the shore break is extremely powerful and there is a very dangerous rip current. Swimming here is not recommended, unless the water is very calm, I repeat, due to the current. This current, the Hala'ea Current, even has a story.

Once there was a chief of this area named Hala'ea. Back in those days, the commoners were obliged to support the ali'i by providing food, mats, etc, much as today we are obliged to pay taxes. This particular chief was greedy, and at the end of each day, he would canoe out to the returning fishermen and demand that their hard-earned fish be given to him. He would then wantonly waste the food, feasting and carousing, while the fishermen and their families starved.

The fishermen finally had had enough, and came up with a plan. One day they paddled out to sea as usual, during 'ahi season, and spent the whole day, catching an abundance of fish. When the greedy Hala'ea paddled out to their canoes at the end of the day, demanding the fish as usual, they divided into two groups and came along side his canoe. They began throwing their fish quickly into his canoe, and then paddled away quickly, before Hala'ea discovered that his canoe had swamped. He was carried away by the current, and never seen again.

This story brings up, to me, a very interesting facet of Ka'u. Historically, it was known as *Ka'u makaha*, "fierce and resourceful Ka'u," and its people were believed to have been descendents from a chief and chiefess who were forced to elope to Ka'u. There they prospered and produced many offspring, in spite of the harsh environment. There was even a saying, *Mai ka uka a ke kai, mai kahi pae a kahi pae, he 'ohana wale no*, which means "From upland to sea, from end to end, one family only." In other words, everyone in Ka'u is related.

In olden days, the people of Ka'u were renowned for sometimes "taking the law into their own hands" and ridding themselves of an oppressive chief, which happened very rarely in other parts of the Islands, as the ali'i caste pretty much controlled with an iron fist, so to speak.

I lived and worked in this area for a time as a social worker, and in my profession got to know a lot about the people in the area. The local families still seem, for the most part, to be related. Everyone's a cousin of everyone else. They still share a distinct pride in their dry, windswept, harsh land, even in the face of very hard economic times, especially for this remote area that has few economic opportunities.

You might get a chance to "talk story" with some of the locals right here at Green Sands. If you do, you will most likely notice that they have a sort of "larger than life" aura about them.

Be sure and head back before dark. There is no light out here.

Once back to your car, take the same route back up South Point Road. If you'd like a taste of local grinds, and more insight into the colorful people of this area, turn right (east) at the top of the road onto Highway 19, and drive four miles into the quaint town of Na'alehu. On the right side of the road is "Shaka's," where you can get all sorts of local kau kau. A half block up on the left is the Punalu'u Bakery, famous for their Hawaiian sweet bread.

If you are driving back to Kona, **drive especially carefully** along the hairpin-curves. Ka'u people driving home from work in Kona are in a hurry to get back to their beloved piece of this rock.

This concludes my list of the twenty-two best beaches on the Big Island, many of them some of the very finest beaches in the world. I hope you enjoyed reading about them, and I hope you get to visit them someday soon. Now I would like to say a bit about...

Beach Safety in Hawaii

First and foremost, always obey that old Hawaiian maxim, **"Never turn your back to the sea."**

Heed all warnings and sign postings. Someone took the trouble to alert you to danger. Pay attention.

Rogue waves, and even small waves have been the contributory factors for many accidental drownings. Never, as I have reiterated here again and again, enter rough waters. Pay heed to close shore breaks; even small waves can knock an unwary, off guard person over, resulting in injury or drowning.

Educate yourself and your children about rip currents and undertows, so that if you or they find yourself caught in one, you know how to get out.

If you have children, especially small children, always keep them near you when at the beach. Never wander away when you think they are safely sleeping in the sand, as a friend of mine did. Her child woke up and decided to take a swim all by herself. Tragically, she drowned at Makalawena.

Never swim alone. Always go with a buddy.

Don't drink alcohol and swim.

Be careful of getting an overdose of sun. With the gentle and cool trade winds here, it's easy to forget you are in the tropics. It's easy to get severely burned.

Tsunamis, tidal waves, are rare but do occur. Near towns, we have warning systems, but if you are far out, perhaps camping, you won't hear them. If you feel an earthquake, leave the beach area and head upslope immediately.

Watch out for ubiquitous sea urchins, wana. They are in most tide pools and on rocks. Their spines are painful and you may end up going to the hospital to get them out. Never poke your fingers in rocks or crevasses; not only might eels be lurking there, but wana are more often there than not. Always place your palm flat handed on rocks when going into or getting out of the water.

Besides eels and wana, there are other dangerous marine animals. Do not handle beautiful cone shells; they have a poisonous dart. Coral can inflict abrasions and lacerations that can lead to severe infection—I know someone who had to have a foot amputated because of an infected coral cut.

Do not walk or stand on coral, no matter if you see other people doing it. Be aware of the possibility of Portuguese Man-o'-War, especially at the far north beaches.

And last but not least—sharks. Attacks do occur, and you might be surprised to know that they average two or three attacks per year. The good news is that attacks are rarely fatal. Of the approximately 40 species of sharks in Hawaiian waters, about eight species come near shore. **They detect sounds and smells up to two miles.** That's a long ways. They are aware of you before you are aware of them.

Don't go into the water at dawn, dusk, or night, or on stormy days, when sharks come inshore to feed. Don't enter the water if you have open or bleeding wounds. Avoid murky water, harbor entrances and the mouths of streams. Don't wear shiny jewelry or high-contrast clothing. Don't splash or swim erratically. If you see fish or turtles behaving strangely, be alert for sharks. Don't swim near spear fishers.

And of course, never provoke a shark!

Chances are, you will never see one. I've seen only one, a baby, in thirty years in Hawaiian waters.

If you are given to hiking, be aware of the danger of lava tubes. They can be overgrown with brush and thus hidden. They can be quite deep.

Malama pono.

(Take care.)

Mahalo!

Mahalo nui, thank you very much, for reading my guide to the best beaches on the Big Island of Hawaii. I truly hope you have a most wonderful time visiting this lovely, this very special place on our planet, and I hope you get to come again. Maybe I'll see you at the beach!

True dreams are born of sea spray.
(Old Hawaiian proverb).

Aloha!

There's no other place that I'd rather be
Than home in these islands
In the middle of the sea.
(Henry Kapono)

***

Discover other titles by Uldra Johnson:

Bones of Love, Stories of Old Hawaii

Hula Angel

Chalice of Love

The Insider's Guide to Hawaii Volcanoes National Park, The Best Things to See and Do at Kilauea Volcano, Including Volcano Village

The Cry Room

Ghosts in the Palm of My Hand

How the Universe Made Love to Petal Andersohn
(Petal Andersohn)

Spiritual Not Religious

Made in the USA
Coppell, TX
22 June 2020